Teacher-Made Assessments

How to Connect Curriculum, Instruction, and Student Learning

Christopher R. Gareis
and Leslie W. Grant

EYE ON EDUCATION
6 DEPOT WAY WEST, SUITE 106
LARCHMONT, NY 10538
(914) 833–0551
(914) 833–0761 fax
www.eyeoneducation.com

Library of Congress Cataloging-in-Publication Data

Gareis, Christopher R.
Teacher-made assessments : how to connect curriculum, instruction, and student learning / Christopher R. Gareis and Leslie W. Grant.
p.cm.
ISBN 978-1-59667-081-5
1. Educational tests and measurements. I. Grant, Leslie W., 1968- II. Title.

LB3051.G28 2008
371.27'1--dc22

2007053026

10 9 8 7 6 5 4 3

Also Available from EYE ON EDUCATION

**Differentiated Assessment
for Middle and High School Classrooms**
Deborah Blaz

**Formative Assessment for English Language Arts:
A Guide for Middle and High School Teachers**
Amy Benjamin

**Short Cycle Assessment:
Improving Student Achievement Through Formative Assessment**
Susan Lang, Todd Stanley and Betsy Moore

**Performance-Based Learning and Assessment
in Middle School Science**
K. Michael Hibbard

**Assessment in Middle and High School Mathematics:
A Teacher's Guide**
Daniel Brahier

**What Every Teacher Needs
to Know about Assessment**
Leslie Walker Wilson

**Teaching, Learning, and Assessment Together:
The Reflective Classroom**
Arthur K. Ellis

**Classroom Instruction from A to Z:
How to Promote Student Learning**
Barbara R. Blackburn

**But I'm Not a Reading Teacher:
Strategies for Literacy Instruction in the Content Areas**
Amy Benjamin

**Handbook on Differentiated Instruction
for Middle and High Schools**
Sheryn Spencer Northey

**Differentiating by Student Learning Preferences:
Strategies and Lesson Plans**
Joni Turville

**Differentiated Instruction for K-8 Math and Science:
Activities and Lesson Plans**
Mary Hamm and Dennis Adams

About the Authors

Christopher R. Gareis, EdD, is associate professor of educational leadership and associate dean for teacher education at the College of William and Mary in Virginia. He teaches courses in instructional leadership, classroom assessment, program evaluation, curriculum development, and instructional strategies. Chris began his career as a high school English teacher, taught at the middle school level, and also served as an assistant principal and principal. Chris regularly works with school districts in the areas of classroom assessment, mentoring, instructional leadership, and teacher evaluation. His publications include articles and books on the topics of teacher portfolios, online mentoring, teacher compensation, and assessment. Chris earned his bachelor's degree in English and East Asian Studies from Washington and Lee University, master's degree in English education from the College of William and Mary, and doctoral degree in educational leadership also from William and Mary.

Leslie W. Grant, PhD, serves as a visiting assistant professor in curriculum and instruction at the College of William and Mary, where she teaches in the teacher preparation program. Leslie has been a teacher, an instructional leader, and a content editor and item writer for a major test publishing company. She earned her doctoral degree in educational policy, planning, and leadership from the College of William and Mary.

Acknowledgements

A project like this book is never simply the product of the work of the names on the front cover. Our understandings, conceptualizations, and even our way of sharing our thinking in writing have undoubtedly been shaped by countless others, far too numerous to acknowledge here by name. We recognize and value the influences of our own teachers—from kindergarten through graduate school—who have been instrumental in shaping who we are as thinkers, researchers, and writers. We also recognize and value the tremendous influences of the many teachers and school leaders with whom we have worked in school and district settings. These colleagues and friends helped shaped us as practitioners, and we hope that we have been true to our school-based roots with this book.

We also thank our students, most especially the many undergraduate and graduate students with whom we have worked in the School of Education at the College of William and Mary. These talented and committed individuals are comprised of aspiring preservice teachers as well as experienced teachers preparing for formal leadership roles in schools and school districts. Their questions, explorations, and insights in the context of our classes have immeasurably contributed to our own learning. In particular, we want to thank the six graduate students—all expert teachers in their own right—who wrote and contributed the Teacher-to-Teacher excerpts in Chapter 2: Lindsey Caccavale, Karen Cagle, Nate Leach, Katie Moore, Charley Shrack, and Ann Vinson. Thank you, all.

We would also like to thank two gentlemen who respectively represent the ideation and the realization of this book: James Stronge and Bob Sickles. James, who is an internationally noted scholar and speaker, has been a support to us both throughout our careers; and he provided the moral encouragement to pursue this project before the first word was ever written. You might say he envisioned this book before even we did. And, if that is the case of James, then it is Bob Sickles of Eye On Education who has brought that vision to realization. Bob has been a gracious and understanding publisher, and he provided valuable support throughout the project. Thank you, both.

Finally, an endeavor of this magnitude would not have been possible without the support of our families. Our loved ones encouraged us to take on this challenge and supported us throughout the writing process. Leslie would like to thank her husband, Allen, and son, Matthew, for their understanding during many, many late nights of writing. She also thanks her mother, sisters, and friends for their words of encouragement. Chris would like to thank his wife, Molly, and their children, Hance, Isabelle, and Anne Ryan, for being blessed reminders of the most important things in life. Chris also thanks his mom, dad, sisters, and brother for continuing to be his deep anchoring roots.

Table of Contents

1

Why Should I Assess Student Learning in My Classroom?

Teaching, Learning. . .and Assessment

How Do You Define *Teaching*?

Take a moment to reflect on how you define this term that we, as teachers, use so often. Chances are that your definition of *teaching* in some way includes mention of another term: namely, *learning*. That's because the act of teaching is not complete until learning has occurred. It's similar to the age-old rhetorical question: "If a tree falls in the forest and there is no one there to hear it, does it make a sound?" We in the education field may well ponder a similar question: "If a teacher teaches but no students have learned, has the teacher taught?" This question helps bring to light an important point: *Learning* is integral to the act of *teaching*.

When we learn, we change. That change may be in something we know, something we're able to do, or something that we believe or value. Thus, as you consider how to define teaching, you must also consider teaching's *results*, and how teaching brings about those results. With this in mind, we define **teaching** as the intentional creation and enactment of activities and experiences by one person that lead to changes in the knowledge, skills, and/or dispositions of another person. Note that our definition does not presume that students are blank slates on which a teacher writes. In fact, we view learning as the creation of meaning both by and within an individual. More specifically, we define **learning** as a relatively permanent change in knowledge, skills, and/or dispositions precipitated by planned or unplanned experiences, events, activities, or interventions. Thus, for the act of teaching to be complete, it must result in learning within another.

Assessment and Learning

As obvious as the relationship between teaching and learning may be, what is less obvious is the *evidence* of learning. For example, when a young child learns to walk, the evidence of learning may be quite clear: We see the child walking; therefore, we know she has learned. This is true of all physical skills: We can quite literally *see* the learned behavior. However, in schools, most of our learning objectives for students are cognitive in nature rather than psychomotor. In other words, so much of what we teach in schools and what students are to learn resides in the mind and is *not* as apparent as a child walking.

So if teaching necessarily involves learning, an important corollary follows: How do teachers know what their students have learned? Teachers need some way of *seeing* learning.

The way teachers see student learning is through a process known as assessment; and assessment, like teaching, is integrally related to our definition of learning. We define **assessment** as the process of using methods or tools to collect information about student learning. In other words, assessment is the way teachers see their students' learning.

Assessment and Teaching: The Light Bulb

There's a familiar image that teachers use to describe one of the most rewarding phenomena in teaching: the light bulb. Perhaps you've used the expression yourself. You're teaching a concept that is difficult for students to grasp. You attempt to get at it one way, then you explain it in another way. You have the students wrestle with the concept, and you have them try to apply it. Then, you begin to see an almost imperceptible change in the facial expression of a student or two. You scaffold the class's thinking and provide encouragement and feedback. One student says, "Oh, I get it!" Another student's eyes seem to say, "Ah-ha!" The *light bulbs* are turning on. One by one, students grasp the concept. And you, as the teacher, rely on their facial expressions, body language, and incidental comments as information about student learning. In other words, you are assessing, albeit informally, student learning in your classroom.

Teachers—at least the truly excellent ones—are teachers because they derive so much personal satisfaction not from their teaching per se, but from other people's learning.[1] Teachers are driven by a desire to make a positive difference in the lives of others by helping others grow, develop, and constructively evolve into their potential as individuals. Whether it's through teaching a first grader to read, mentoring a middle school student through a personal crisis while still managing to help him master fractions, or engendering a passion for historical research in a high school student, teaching is the conveyance of knowledge and the fostering of skills in ways that become enabling of and meaningful to the learner. It's this motivation for others *to learn* that seems to be at the core of why teachers *teach*. Central to this relationship between teaching and learning is the ability of a teacher to *discern* that students are, in fact, learning. In other words, assessment—whether informal or formal—is the means by which a teacher knows what students are or are not learning. Assessment is integral to teaching.

Curriculum, Instruction...and Assessment

In a formal educational setting such as a school, the act of teaching and learning is comprised of two essential components: curriculum and instruction. **Curriculum** is a set of intentionally identified outcomes of learning.[2] Put more plainly, curriculum is *what* we intend for students to know, be able to do, and value as a result of learning. It follows then that instruction is the means—or the *how*—of curriculum. **Instruction** is comprised of the planned and unplanned experiences provided by a teacher that are intended to result in the acquisition of a set of intended learning outcomes for students. In short, for teachers in schools, curriculum and instruction are the stuff of teaching and learning.

However, curriculum and instruction alone represent an incomplete model of teaching and learning in the classroom. In addition to knowing *what* to teach and *how* to teach it, a teacher must also be able to discern *the degree to which* students have learned at any given point in time. Figure 1.1 represents these three elements as a single, unified whole.

Figure 1.1. A Model of Curriculum, Instruction, and Assessment

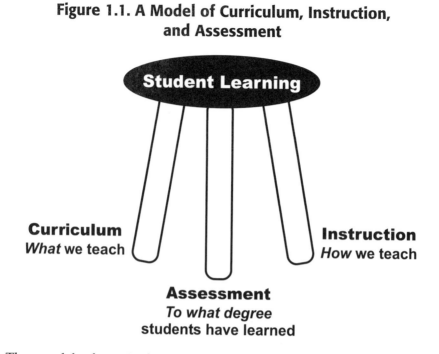

Student Learning

Curriculum
What we teach

Instruction
How we teach

Assessment
To what degree
students have learned

The model of curriculum, instruction, and assessment illustrates the integrated nature of the teaching and learning process. Teaching is *not* a singular event in which teaching perfectly and inevitably leads to learning. Rather, teaching is a recursive activity that relies on teachers to determine accurately what students are learning, to what degree they are learning, and what they are *not* learning. Teaching relies on teachers' ability to collect information about student learning to make decisions about what to teach and how to teach next. In other words, assessment is integral to decisions that classroom teachers must make about both instruction and curriculum.

Understanding the integrated nature of curriculum, instruction, and assessment is one of the important foundations of effective teaching.[3,] However, although many teachers can grasp this notion, it seems that assessment in the classroom is often unintentionally devalued. Consider some of the common misconceptions about assessment made by classroom teachers, shown in Figure 1.2.

Figure 1.2. Teacher Voices: Common Misconceptions About Assessment in the Classroom

"I give tests because I've gotta give grades."

"Tests are a necessary evil: I hate giving them and students hate taking them."

"Assessments don't have anything to do with teaching and learning."

"Standardized assessments only test lower-level thinking."

"Assessing students is easy: It's just a matter of asking questions."

Although there are certainly others, these common misconceptions about assessment in the classroom illustrate how the seemingly intuitive relationship among curriculum, instruction, and assessment (see Figure 1.1) can falter when teachers fail to grasp the various roles of assessment in the classroom. Without assessment, the act of teaching becomes a process focused only on the teachers' inputs of curriculum and instruction, as illustrated in Figure 1.3. Without assessment, student learning becomes absent from the teaching-and-learning process. If assessment is the means to discern student learning, then, in its absence, teaching becomes all about teachers and their decisions and *not* about the students and their needs or their learning. Similar to the two-legged stool in Figure 1.3, teaching without some means of assessment—that is, some means of determining the degree and nature of student learning—is about as dependable as a two-legged stool.

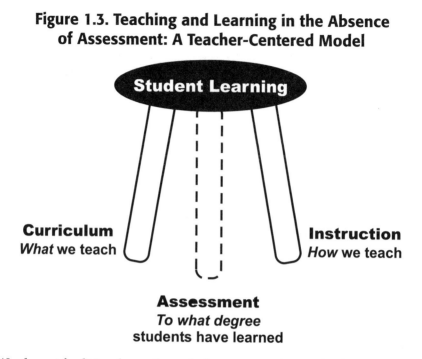

Figure 1.3. Teaching and Learning in the Absence of Assessment: A Teacher-Centered Model

We do not fault teachers, though. In our experiences both as teachers and in working with teachers, assessment in the classroom is most often misused not for a want of conceptual understanding about the need to determine student learning but for want of a technical understanding about how to appropriately create and use assessments in the classroom. We begin to explore this next. Indeed, the focus and intent of this book is to help teachers to be better creators and users of assessment—specifically, paper-and-pencil tests—by understanding the basic principles and techniques of assessment.

The Roles of Assessment in the Classroom

There are three fundamental roles of assessment in the classroom, and they are oftentimes distinguished by *when* they occur in relation to instruction:

1. **Preassessment** is the assessment of student learning prior to teaching

2. **Formative assessment** is the assessment of student learning integrated into the act of teaching

3. **Summative assessment** is the assessment of student learning at the end of some period of instruction

Figure 1.4 provides a side-by-side comparison of preassessment, formative assessment, and summative assessment across a number of facets, including why to assess, when to assess, what to assess, and how to assess. This overview is intended to provide a basic comparison of the roles of assessment in the classroom and to distinguish each of the roles from the others.

Although this type of overview can be helpful, we caution teachers about interpreting Figure 1.4 too literally. In the day-to-day life of teachers, the fact is that the roles of assessment in the classroom oftentimes overlap. A seventh-grade teacher, for example, may decide to use a discrepant event, such as students' observation of a three-leafed clover and a four-leafed clover, as a way to begin an inquiry-based model of instruction for a unit on genetics. During the portion of the activity when students are following their observations with possible ways to investigate the phenomenon, the teacher may informally assess students' abilities to generate hypotheses.[4] In this situation, the teacher is using an activity that serves as both a preassessment of students' prior learning as well as a formative assessment to make decisions about the direction of the day's instruction.

Figure 1.4. Comparison of the Three Roles of Assessment in the Classroom

Key Questions	Preassessment *Before* instruction	Formative *During* instruction	Summative *After* instruction
When does assessment occur?	*Before* instruction	*During* instruction	*After* instruction
Why assess?	To determine prior knowledge and/or entering skills of students	To make instructional decisions	To judge the degree and/or worth of student learning
What is the **extent** of an assessment's coverage?	Either *focused* or *comprehensive*, depending on the intended use	*Focused* on discrete knowledge or a particular skill set	*Comprehensive* of some period of instruction and some set of knowledge and/or skills
What are the typical **consequential outcomes** of an assessment?	*High stakes* if used for placement decisions; *Low stakes* if used for instructional planning	*Low stakes:* typically related to day-to-day decisions about teaching and learning	*High stakes:* can determine future placement, remediation, honors designations, and so forth
Who primarily uses the results of the assessment?	Teacher	Teacher and students	Teacher, students, and third parties (such as parents, administrators, and guidance counselors)
How is the assessment typically done?	• Pretests • Interviews • Class discussions • Reviews of cumulative records	• Observations of facial expressions, body language, and incidental comments • Q&A, with students responding by hand raising, thumbs up/down, personal response systems, and so forth • In-class guided practice • Homework assignments • Paper-and-pencil quizzes	• Paper-pencil tests, quizzes, essays, and papers • Projects, demonstrations, performances, and original creations • Standardized tests

By way of a second example, consider the classic tenth-grade term paper in an English class. Clearly, a term paper—as suggested by the very name itself—is a comprehensive assessment of knowledge and skills developed over the course of an academic term. In this regard, a term paper is a summative assessment, and it often carries great weight in determining a student's grade for a marking period. Conversely, the process of researching and writing the term paper is typically undertaken over a considerable period of time, with much direction and feedback from the teacher as each student completes various stages of the project, such as identifying a focused topic, conducting research, and developing a theme, followed by drafting, composing, and editing the paper itself. These processes and intermittent deadlines, as well as the teacher's close oversight, direction, and feedback to each student, constitute a series of formative assessments through which the student both gives evidence of her learning *and* refines her learning. Thus, the classic tenth-grade English term paper suggests that assessments may serve roles that are both formative and summative.

With these two examples in mind, Figure 1.5 represents a more practical view of the three roles of assessment in the classroom. In this model, classroom assessment is viewed as a continuum along which the distinctions that separate preassessment from formative assessment or formative assessment from summative assessment become blurred. We go so far as to suggest that, in a manner of speaking, all classroom assessment is formative in nature in the following way: *All classroom assessment of student learning is intended ultimately to contribute to and to result in improving student learning.* It is vital that a teacher, to be as effective as possible, understands and appreciates not only the various roles of assessment but also its ultimate purpose in teaching and learning. Assessment matters to teaching and learning.

Figure 1.5. The Continuum of Classroom Assessment

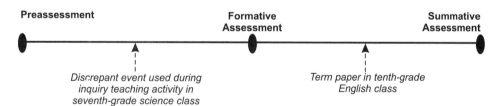

Assessment Matters:
Improving Student Learning

Although the role of assessment in teaching has long been understood, what has been less evident is the effect that assessment practices in the classroom can have on the quality of teaching and the improvement of student learning. Does assessment matter in improving student learning? Research in recent years suggests that it does. Consider some of the research findings about assessment:

- ◆ Improved formative assessment practices in classrooms typically yield gains in student achievement roughly equivalent to one to two grade levels in learning.[5]

- ◆ Teachers' regular use of multiple choice format—although *not* to the exclusion of supply-response assessments such as short-answer or essays—has been correlated with improved student performance on the National Assessment of Educational Progress (NAEP), notably in the area of science.[6]

- ◆ Teachers' use of *providing feedback* to students in the classroom can have statistically significant effects on student achievement.[7]

This sample of recent studies is illustrative of our growing understanding of assessment not only as a *measure* of student learning but also as a *means* to student learning.[8] With all due respect to these researchers, however, the idea is not entirely new. Arguably, the practice of using assessment to improve student learning has been around as long as teaching has. Looking back a couple millennia, we are reminded that Socrates' *modus docendi*—that is, his "preferred way of teaching"—was to *question* the learner. What we now call the Socratic method essentially amounts to the use of questioning to assess students' understanding, guide learning, and, ultimately, foster critical thinking. In other words, the Socratic method is a means of teaching *through assessment*.

Assessment and
the Accountability Movement

The image of Socrates questioning his students on the steps of a public forum in Greece presents a benign image of assessment. Unfortunately, we live in an era today that many teachers consider far from benign. In the public policy arena, the field of education has been strongly buffeted by the forces of the accountability movement.

The emphasis on accountability in education is often traced to the seminal report of the Education Commission of the States published in 1983 titled *A Nation At Risk,* in which public schools in the United States were said to be characterized by a "rising tide of mediocrity."[9] Although schools in the United States have been subject to answering the call of citizens, business leaders, and policymakers to meet the real and perceived needs of society since as far back as Horace Mann's first organization of common schools in the 1800s, *A Nation At Risk* articulated a view for the first time from the federal government that public schools should be held to account for the academic achievement—and even the societal outcomes—of the educational process.

During the ensuing decades between 1983 and 2002, the federal government and the governors of all 50 states moved the nation toward an increasingly defined system of identified educational standards and accountability measures, culminating in the passage of *No Child Left Behind* (NCLB) in 2002.[10] Central to NCLB is its mandate for schools to be accountable for demonstrating that all students—regardless of race, gender, economic status, English language ability, or disability—achieve adequate yearly progress toward meeting a state's respective educational standards. And how do students demonstrate their progress? Through performance on state standardized assessments.

We should say at this point that our aim here is not to argue the relative merits (there are many) and the erroneous assumptions (there are quite a few of these, too) of NCLB as a federal educational policy. Instead, our intent is to point out the effect that NCLB has had on the role of assessment in the classroom. To state the case briefly, the confluence of NCLB's adequate yearly progress requirement, the articulation of state standards of learning, and the profusion of state standardized assessments puts an extraordinary emphasis on assessment as something *external to* the teaching and learning that takes place in the classroom. So, although our purer understanding of teaching and learning has us value assessment as *integral to* the educational process, the current era of accountability has shifted the thinking of many teachers to view assessment as something that is *done to* their students and, by extension, is *done to* teachers, too. In other words, assessment is viewed quite negatively by many teachers in the present day.

Teachers' impressions about state standardized assessments are not without merit. Because state standardized assessments have begun to carry high stakes for individual students, teachers, school leaders, districts, and states, a number of unintended consequences are becoming increasingly evident. Figure 1.6 summarizes some of the most notable, negative effects of high-stakes standardized tests associated with the accountability movement.

There's little question that the unintended consequences shared in Figure 1.6 constitute negative effects on our public education system. However, it's not our position that standardized assessments should be abandoned, nor do we advocate a wholesale dismantling of NCLB. Standardized assessments, when administered and used properly, can provide valuable information regarding a student's, a school's, and a school district's progress relative to some important outcomes. Instead, we strongly believe that informed, professional judgment should guide the substantive revision of both policy and practice regarding standardized assessments. Indeed, one of the aims of this book is to contribute to the diffusion of professional knowledge about assessment among aspiring and practicing teachers so that teachers can be excellent creators of classroom-based assessments and excellent consumers of standardized assessments. With this in mind, it is helpful to consider how both types of assessments—that is, classroom-based and standardized assessments—contribute to the process of finding out about student learning. Figure 1.7 presents a side-by-side comparison that helps to illustrate the positive and complementary roles that the two types of assessments play.

We should note that in Figure 1.7 (p. 15.) we have looked at both standardized and classroom-based assessments in a decidedly positive way. To be sure, there can be drawbacks to either. However, neither standardized tests nor classroom-based assessments alone is sufficient to meet the need of teachers to accurately and dependably gauge and thereby support continued student learning. Again, we contend that teachers must have proficient understanding and ability to employ both.

Figure 1.6. Negative Unintended Consequences of High-Stakes Standardized Tests

Unintended Consequence	Explanation [11, 12]
Lack of test validity leads to incomplete and inaccurate inferences about student learning	Not all standards can be assessed on objective standardized tests; therefore, results on these tests can lead to inaccurate inferences about what students truly know or are able to do.[11] Consider, as examples, these educational outcomes: • The student designs and conducts an original scientific experiment. • The student researches and composes a factually based interpretation of historical events. • The student creates, orally presents, and defends a persuasive argument. Such outcomes are unarguably complex and represent the highest levels of cognitive behavior, yet standardized tests are incapable of assessing a student's mastery of them. Would anyone want to draw conclusions about a student's learning of science, history, or language arts without some such performance? We imagine not. Thus, in short, *standardized tests ultimately provide incomplete representations of educational outcomes.*
The curriculum is narrowed	Continuing from the preceding explanation, when the standards that are actually assessed on a high-stakes test are narrowed because some standards (oftentimes the most important standards) are simply not conducive to being assessed in a multiple choice format, there is the danger that teachers will teach primarily—if not exclusively—to the standards that are tested. This over-focus on the tested standards can result in increased test preparation and a focus on breadth rather than depth.[12] Even more damaging can be the effect that some important curricular objectives do not get taught at all. Some teachers rationalize that it is better to over-teach a tested standard than to teach a nontested standard. After all, teachers are not externally judged on students' performance on the nontested standards. And, on a larger scale, schools and school districts make the decision to drop courses in nontested subject areas such as art or music from the curriculum altogether!

Figure 1.6 continues on next page.

Figure 1.6. Continued
[13,14,15]

Unintended Consequence	Explanation
Lack of test reliability leads to undependable inferences about student learning	State standardized tests are intentionally designed to assess hundreds of thousands of students at a time in as objective a manner as possible and to report results to state and district officials and to the public as quickly as possible. Typically, high-stakes tests consist of 25 to 50 or so multiple choice questions per subject area. The reliability of such tests (that is, the degree to which we can depend on a student's score being an accurate indication of their learning) is threatened by certain limitations. First, the limited number of items on a test (for example, 30 questions to assess an entire school year of instruction in fourth-grade math) means that a content strand within a subject area may be assessed by one or two questions on the test. If a student misses (or gets correct) one of these two questions purely by chance, an inaccurate impression of student learning is formed. Second, standardized assessments are single measures in time. Although we administer tests year after year, the fact is that an individual student's score on a test represents his learning at one single point in time. Standardized tests do not provide for repeated measures to gauge the consistency of a student's performance over time. Thus, if a student performs poorly on testing day purely by chance, illness, unrequited love, or any other of a hundred reasons, the impression of his learning is, again, undependable.
Some people resort to cheating	A cursory review of a few major newspapers makes this point disappointingly obvious: • A director of testing is accused of changing student answer sheets and filling in unanswered questions.[13] • Principals and teachers in five states resign after improperly aiding students on state exams.[14] • Teachers are investigated in cheating probe in Texas.[15] Of course, we could well argue that cheating is as prevalent in classroom assessment as it is in these cases. However, it is important to remember that cheating in these cases is oftentimes conspiratorial (that is, involving several people) and involves adult professionals who are willing to risk their livelihood and, in the case of criminal conviction, their very freedom to falsify results. High stakes, indeed.

Figure 1.7. The Roles of Standardized and Classroom-Based Assessments

Standardized Assessments Can Provide...	Classroom Assessments Can Provide...
Standardized conditions and, therefore, *comparison* among students, schools, districts, and even states	*Tailored* or *unique* assessments, which take into account the particular characteristics of students and the specific contextual factors of a classroom or school setting
Annual assessment information, which is indicative of *prevailing trends* among a population one year to the next	*Timely assessment information*, which is indicative of student learning over a particular instructional unit and progress toward mastery of either discrete or broad-reaching objectives
Validity in that they are typically aligned with the *formal state curriculum*	*Validity* in that they are typically more responsive to the *taught curriculum*— that is, the objectives that students actually had the opportunity to learn through instruction
Reliability in that they are typically constructed to be delivered under highly controlled conditions, objectively graded, and systematically subjected to reviews to eliminate ineffective or inappropriate items	*Greater authenticity* in that classroom-based assessments often take the form of assignments that tap depth of content and breadth of skills—assignments such as extended writing and essays, individual projects, group-based projects, labs, demonstrations, and performances
Summative assessments of learning that are indicative of achievement of a comprehensive set of knowledge and/or skills, typically inclusive of a year or more of instruction	*Formative* assessments, the results of which may be used to provide timely feedback to students and to allow teachers to make instructional decisions to support continued learning
High-stakes evaluation information that can be used to make judgments about the degree and/or quality of student, teacher, school, district, and/or state performance	*Low-stakes* (relatively speaking) evaluation information that can be used to communicate the degree and quality of learning to students, parents, teachers, and other education professionals

Assessment as a Professional Competency

Inarguably, assessment is playing an increasingly central role in education. Therefore, the imperative for teachers to understand and employ classroom-based assessments and standardized assessments is greater than ever before. Teachers must be as proficient in the area of assessment as they have traditionally been in the areas of curriculum and instruction. Indeed, we strongly contend that assessment must be viewed as a professional competency that every teacher should be compelled to develop and demonstrate for purposes of licensure. We're not alone in this thought. A review of state licensure standards for teachers illustrates the value placed on assessment as a professional competency. Figure 1.8 presents several examples of language from state licensure standards.

We should reiterate that the states presented in Figure 1.8 represent a random sample and that similar language is found in the licensure regulations among all 50 states. We should also note that we've presented excerpts only. In a number of states, the general language regarding assessment (as presented in Figure 1.8) is followed by relatively specific subcompetencies that address the particular knowledge and skills that are inherent to "using a variety of formal and informal assessment strategies," as many of the licensure regulations state.

At the risk of oversimplifying a complex professional competency, we contend that there are three core principles regarding teachers' competency in the area of assessment. Fundamentally, teachers must be proficient at *creating, consuming,* and *communicating about* assessments in their classrooms. These ideas are explored further in Chapter 7, but mentioning these three fundamental ways in which teachers work with assessment is important as we explore the professional practice of assessment in Chapters 2 through 6.

Figure 1.8. Sample Language From
State Teacher Licensure Regulations Regarding Assessment

State	Excerpted Language From Licensure Regulations
Alabama[16]	The candidate understands and uses formal and informal assessment strategies to evaluate student progress.
Florida[17]	Knowledge of various types of assessment strategies that can be used to determine student levels and needs.
Georgia[18]	Teachers understand and use a range of formal and informal assessment strategies to evaluate and ensure the continuous development of all learners.
Missouri[19]	The preservice teacher understands and uses formal and informal assessment strategies to evaluate and ensure the continuous intellectual, social, and physical development of the learner.
New Mexico[20]	The teacher effectively utilizes student assessment techniques and procedures. . . . (A) Uses a variety of assessment tools and strategies. (B) Uses information gained from ongoing assessment for remediation and instructional planning. (C) Maintains documentation of student progress. (D) Communicates student progress to students and families in a timely manner.
Oklahoma[21]	The teacher understands and uses a variety of assessment strategies to evaluate and modify the teaching/learning process ensuring the continuous intellectual, social and physical development of the learner.
Rhode Island[22]	Teachers use a variety of formal and informal assessment strategies to support the continuous development of the learner.
Vermont[23]	The educator uses multiple assessment strategies to evaluate student growth and modify instruction to ensure continuous intellectual, social, physical, and emotional development of every student.
Wisconsin[24]	The teacher understands and uses formal and informal assessment strategies to evaluate and ensure the continuous intellectual, social, and physical development of the pupil.

The Purpose of this Book:
Developing Teachers' Competency in Test-Making

How did most practicing classroom teachers learn how to assess student learning? There seem to be some typical scenarios:

- Some of us learned everything we know about assessing student learning because we were once students! In other words, we formed our understanding of how to assess students based on our past experiences taking tests and quizzes ourselves.

- Many of us completed one or more courses in instructional methods as part of our teacher preparation programs, and assessment was covered—to some degree or another—within the context of those courses. However, it may also have been that assessment was given a good deal less attention than was given to issues of curriculum planning and instructional delivery. Assessment in such courses is often given short shrift, if for no other reason than lack of time.

- For others, our formal training in assessment occurred within the context of a course in educational testing and measurement. But oftentimes in such courses, the focus is on the psychometric principles of assessment that, while important, are not necessarily translated into practical usage in the classroom.

Of course, there are others among us who have had the benefit of formal and effective preparation through a course or through professional development experiences. However, in our own personal and professional experiences as teachers and working with teachers, individuals with such preparation are *not* the norm. This isn't a condemnation of these teachers. (In fact, we are two teachers among those with little formal preparation prior to entering the classroom.) Rather, our anecdotal experiences with teachers have illuminated for us the need in the profession for current classroom teachers to develop their knowledge and skills in the area of assessment.

But our anecdotal impressions are not enough to undertake our writing (and your reading!) of an entire book on the topic. So, we look to other evidence of this need:

- The emphasis on assessment as a core teacher competency is relatively new. In 1983 a survey of state teacher certification standards revealed that only 10 states specifically required course work in assessment. The same was true in a follow-up study of requirements in 1989.[25]

- As of the year 2000, only 14 states explicitly required demonstrated competence in assessment for teacher licensure, and only three required it of administrators.[26] That means there's a strong likelihood that most current teachers who completed their professional preparation 10 to 30 years ago have gaps in their knowledge and skills regarding assessment.

♦ Similarly, the *Student Evaluation Standards,* which were developed by the Joint Committee on Standards for Educational Evaluation, were not published until 2003.[27] These are an extraordinary resource to teachers and other education professionals (and we address them in detail in Chapter 2), but they are relatively new to the field. Therefore, as a field, we are very much in the early stages of seeing dissemination of the standards and their effect on practice.

♦ Research in the field suggests that assessment as a competency is an area of relative discomfort, if not weakness, among teachers. In one study, researchers reviewed teachers' professional portfolios, which documented performance in five domains of teacher responsibility, including planning for instruction, instructional delivery, assessment of student learning, classroom management, and professionalism. Of these five domains, assessment was the area *least* adequately documented among teachers.[28]

♦ Educational reformers have identified assessment as a gap in the professional practice of classroom teachers. Mike Schmoker, for example, drew the following observation based on his breadth of experiences working with schools and observing in classrooms across the United States: "[It] became apparent that student assessment was surprisingly rare and haphazard. Students would spend days, even weeks, on activities without being assessed. A surprising proportion of student work was handed in but never returned—or returned weeks later, often without written feedback, and with no chance to revise."[29]

♦ Research also suggests that assessment as a competency rarely seems to be the focus of professional development. One study found that barely more than half of all science teachers in the sample (53%) had received any type of professional development on performance-based assessment, whether an hour-long workshop, a three-credit graduate level course, or any other professional development format. The findings were more disconcerting among mathematics teachers because only 38% reported receiving any such professional development.[30]

♦ Even among new teachers, research suggests assessment is an area of need. In a recent study of first-year teachers, assessment was the weakest competency on average when compared to the competencies of novice teachers in instructional delivery and classroom management.[31]

From this brief review of findings from the field and from our own experiences both as teachers and working with classroom teachers, it is evident to us that many teachers can gain from improving their professional knowledge and skills in the area of classroom-based assessment. In short, therefore, this book aims to help teachers become more competent creators, consumers, and communicators about classroom-based assessments—with a very specific focus on paper-and-pencil classroom-based tests—to promote and support student learning.

Our audience for this book is, first and foremost, the classroom teacher. As former classroom teachers ourselves, we well recognize that you are busy . . . very, very busy. You have 20 to 200 students to attend to in a given day. You have parents with whom to communicate; noninstructional duties intended to contribute to the smooth running of the school; and, somewhere in there, personal lives and responsibilities, too. So, we sought to write a book that provides essential information, develops practical skills, and is written in what we hope is a professional but accessible style.

We should point out that this book is not a comprehensive tome on educational assessment, and it is not a scholarly epistle intended to change the way the profession views assessment. There are places for such works, and there are many excellent examples of them available to you. In fact, we reference quite a few throughout this book. But we have worked to write a book for current (and even aspiring) classroom teachers who are seeking to improve their ability to determine what their students learned from them yesterday, or during the past week, or this semester. Our aim is to help teachers become even more proficient and more confident in their assessment of student learning in their own classrooms. To that end, we focus our discussion and examples on teacher-made, classroom-based tests. A **test,** as we are using the term in this book, is a deliberately designed, representative set of written questions and/or prompts to which students respond in written form, intended to measure the acquisition of certain knowledge, skills, and/or dispositions. Admittedly, this is a rather weighty definition. But, the basic concept of what a classroom test is intended to do is simple enough: A teacher's test is intended to determine the nature and degree of student learning, and a test is intended to do so in a way that is both meaningful and practical. Given the prevalence of tests as the primary means of determining student learning, our focus is on the characteristics of and basic principles for constructing good tests for the classroom. However, the principles and techniques presented throughout this book can be applied to performance-based forms of assessment, as well.

Finally, we should also explain our larger aim with this book. Simply put, our intention is to influence the professional practice of as many teachers as we can so that they can ultimately teach more effectively; and, therefore, their students can learn more successfully and more meaningfully. In other words, we hope we can teach teachers—including preservice teachers—something useful and valuable through this book. And we hope it helps teachers, in turn, to teach useful and valuable things to their students.

Overview of the Book

This book is intended to be a practical and accessible resource for classroom teachers as they align their own tests and quizzes with the content and format expected of state and district standards-based curricula. The book is organized into seven chapters. Chapters 1 and 2 provide a rationale for the focus of the book, and lay a foundational understanding of key principles of assessment, including validity and reliability. (Some readers may find an inductive approach to developing valid and reliable assessments by beginning with Chapter 1 and reading through to the end. Others may prefer a deductive approach, beginning with the practical applications in Chapters 3, 4, 5 and then reading Chapters 1, 2, 6 and 7.) Chapter 3 presents the process of constructing assessments as 10 basic steps, and it illustrates the critical task of unpacking a standards-based curriculum and designing classroom-based tests that are aligned in content as well as in the level of cognitive demand expected of students. Chapter 4 explains and illustrates how to construct select-response items, with a particular focus on multiple choice items, whereas Chapter 5 explains and illustrates the construction of supply-response items, with special attention to short answer and essay prompts and the development of scoring rubrics. Chapter 6 describes the crucial role of feedback in making use of classroom test results to support student learning. Finally, Chapter 7 expands the focus of the book by describing a number of specific ways in which classroom teachers—equipped with meaningful understandings of the purposes and means of appropriate classroom assessment—can constructively influence the professional practice of other teachers in their schools and districts.

1   Stronge, J. H. (2002). *Qualities of effective teachers.* Alexandria, VA: Association for Supervision and Curriculum Development.

2   Johnson, M. (2004). Definitions and models in curriculum theory. In Ornstein, A. C., & Hunkins, F. P. *Curriculum: Foundations, principles, and issues* (4th ed., p. 180). New York: Pearson.

3   Marzano, R. J. (2003). *What works in schools.* Alexandria, VA: Association for Supervision and Curriculum Development; Stronge (2002).

4   Joyce B., Weil, M., & Calhoun, E. (2000). *Models of teaching.* Boston: Allyn & Bacon; Marzano, R. J., Pickering, D., & Pollock, J. (2001). *Classroom instruction that works.* Alexandria, VA: Association for Supervision and Curriculum Development.

5   Assessment Reform Group. (1999). *Assessment for learning: Beyond the black box.* Cambridge: University of Cambridge School of Education.

6   Wenglinsky, H. (2000). *How teaching matters: Bringing the classroom back into discussions of teacher quality.* Princeton, NJ: Educational Testing Service.

7   Marzano, Pickering, & Pollock (2001).

8   Assessment Reform Group. (1999); Wenglinsky, H. (2000); Marzano, Pickering, & Pollock (2001).

9   Education Commission of the States. (1983). *A nation at risk.* Retrieved May 21, 2007, from http://www.ed.gov/pubs/NatAtRisk/risk.html

10   Manna, P. (2006). *School's in: Federalism and the national education agenda.* Washington, DC: Georgetown University Press.

11   Popham, W. J. (2003). Trouble with testing. *American School Board Journal.* Retrieved January 25, 2007, from http://www.nsba.org/site/doc.asp?TRACKID=&CID=1234&DID=33030

12   Clarke, M., Shore, A., Rhoades, K., Abrams, L., Miao, J., & Li, J. (2003). Perceived effects of state-mandated testing programs on teaching and learning: Findings from interviews with educators in low-, medium-, and high-stakes states. *Report from National Board on Educational Testing and Public Policy.* Boston: Boston College.

13   Burney, M. (2007, January 18). Camden's probe: Rigging at Brimm. *The Philadelphia Enquirer.* Retrieved January 22. 2007, from http://callbears.findarticles.com/p/articles/mi_kmtpi/is_200701/ai_n17139934

14   Magnunson, P. (2000). High stakes cheating: Will the focus on accountability lead to more cheating? *Communicator.* Retrieved January 22, 2007, from http://www.naesp.org/ContentLoad.do?contentId=151&action=print

15   Axtman, K. (2005, January 11). When the test's cheaters are the teachers: Probe of Texas scores on high stakes tests is the latest case in a series of cheating incidents. *The Christian Science Monitor.* Retrieved

January 22, 2007, from www.csmonitor.com/2005/0111/p01s03-ussc.htm

16 Alabama Department of Education. Rules of the state board of education, Chapter 290-3-3, Teacher Education. Retrieved January 5, 2007, from ftp://ftp.alsde.edu/documents/66/Code051105SB. doc

17 Florida Department of Education. Professional education. Retrieved January 5, 2007, from http://www.firn.edu/ttdoe/sas/ftce/pdf/ftcomp00.pdf

18 Georgia Systemic Teacher Education Program. GSTEP framework guiding principles. Retrieved January 6, 2007, from http://www.coe.uga.edu/gstep/documents/index.html

19 Missouri Department of Elementary and Secondary Education. Missouri Standards for Teacher Education Programs. Retrieved January 19, 2007, from http://dese.mo.gov/divteachqual/teached/Institutional%20Handbook/appendixB.pdf/standards.htm

20 Teach New Mexico. New Mexico teacher competencies. Retrieved March 14, 2007, from http://www.teachnm.org/nm_teacher_competencies.html

21 Oklahoma Commission for Teacher Preparation. General competencies for licensure. Retrieved January 5, 2007, from http://www.octp.org/general_competencies_for_licensure.html

22 Rhode Island Department of Elementary and Secondary Education. Office of educator quality and certification: Rhode Island beginning teacher standards. Retrieved January 19, 2007, from http://www.ridoe.net/educatorquality/certification/bts.aspx

23 Vermont Department of Education. Licensing regulations. Retrieved March 14, 2007, from http://education.vermont.gov/new/pdfdoc/board/rules/5100.pdf

24 Wisconsin Department of Public Instruction. Teacher education program approval and licenses. Retrieved March 14, 2007, from http://dpi.state.wi.us/tepdl/pi34.html#teacherstandards3402

25 Wolmut, P. (1992). On the matter of testing misinformation. A paper presented at the SRA, Inc., Invitational Conference, Phoenix, AZ. In Stiggins, R. J., & Conklin, N. F., *In teachers' hands: Investigating the practices of classroom assessment.* Albany: State University of New York Press.

26 Atkin, J. M., Black, P., & Coffey, J. (Eds.). (2001). *Classroom assessment and the National Science Education Standards* (p. 102). Washington, DC: National Academy Press.

27 Joint Committee on Standards for Educational Evaluation. (2003). *The student evaluation standards: How to improve evaluations of students.* Thousand Oaks, CA: Corwin Press.

28   Tucker, P. D., Stronge, J. H., Gareis, C. R., & Beers, C. S. (2003). The efficacy of portfolios for teacher evaluation and professional development: Do they make a difference? *Educational Administration Quarterly, 39*(5), 572–602.

29   Schmoker, M. (2006). *Results now: How we can achieve unprecedented results in teaching and learning* (p. 86). Alexandria, VA: Association for Supervision and Curriculum Development.

30   Wenglinsky, H. (2000). *How teaching matters: Bringing the classroom back into discussions of teacher quality.* Princeton, NJ: Educational Testing Service.

31   Good, T. L., McCaslin, M., Tsang, H. Y., Zhang, J., Wiley, C. R. H., Bozack, A. R., et al. (2006). How well do 1st-year teachers teach: Does type of preparation make a difference? *Journal of Teacher Education, 57*(4), 410–430.

2

What Makes a Good Test?

As a student, did you ever take a test that you simply thought was unfair? Maybe the questions seemed so complex that you couldn't figure out what was even being asked. Perhaps none of what you studied seemed to be on the test. Maybe you were so distracted by something your friend had shared with you before class that you couldn't concentrate during the test. Whatever the scenario, there were likely some rather predictable results from the test experience. First, your grade on the test was probably not what you hoped it would be. Second, you probably felt frustrated by—and maybe even angry about—the experience. You probably felt your grade on the test did not accurately reflect what you actually knew about the content being tested.

If you have had a similar experience, you understand the basic principles of good assessment in the classroom. Namely, when a teacher uses a test, quiz, project, performance, or some other assessment to determine the nature and degree of student learning, the teacher must ensure that the assessment is both *valid* and *reliable*. These two terms are, no doubt, quite familiar to you. But, as commonplace as the terms are and as frequently as teachers may use them, teachers oftentimes flounder when specifically applying these principles to their own construction and use of assessments in the classroom.

In this chapter, we explore what it means for any assessment, including a teacher-made test, to be valid and reliable. We should point out from the beginning, however, that our intent is neither a comprehensive nor an esoterically nuanced explanation of these concepts. Instead, our intent is to help you refine, if not develop, a *practical* understanding of both validity and reliability so that you can apply these principles in your day-to-day responsibilities as a classroom teacher constructing and using your own assessments. We start by considering validity and reliability in the context of the attributes that should characterize any student assessment—from a teacher-made quiz to a commercially produced standardized test. These essential attributes of a good assessment are identified and described in *The Student Evaluation Standards.*[1]

The Student Evaluation Standards

What makes a really good assessment? In 2003, the Joint Committee on Standards for Educational Evaluation articulated an answer to this question. The Joint Committee was comprised of nearly 20 organizations in the areas of education, assessment, and evaluation. The collective experience and expertise of the members of the Joint Committee and their ability to come to consensus on the attributes of student assessment and evaluation should help us as teachers to feel confident in the product of their work, *The Student Evaluation Standards*.[2] In short, the Joint Committee's Student Evaluation Standards identify four attributes of what we may simply describe as a good assessment. The four attributes are *propriety, utility, feasibility,* and *accuracy*.[3] The Joint Committee's descriptions of each of these essential attributes are presented in Figure 2.1.

Figure 2.1. The Student Evaluation Standards[4]

Four Attributes of Appropriate Assessments	
Propriety	The propriety standards help ensure that student evaluations are conducted legally, ethically, and with due regard for the well-being of the students being evaluated and other people affected by the evaluation results.
Utility	The utility standards help ensure that student evaluations are useful. Useful student evaluations are informative, timely, and influential.
Feasibility	The feasibility standards help ensure that student evaluations can be implemented as planned. Feasible evaluations are practical, diplomatic, and adequately supported.
Accuracy	The accuracy standards help ensure that a student evaluation produces sound information about a student's learning and performance. Sound information leads to valid interpretations, justifiable conclusions, and appropriate follow-up.

Note: The overview of The Student Evaluation Standards originally published by Corwin Press in 2003 is not copyrighted, and the Joint Committee encourages reproduction and dissemination of the standards as presented. Please see the original source in this reference citation for additional information.

Within the four broad categories are 28 specific standards. Each of these 28 standards for student evaluation is presented in the Appendix, and we commend the Joint Committee's use of plain language in expressing the sometimes complex principles that sit behind each standard. We also highly recommend the Joint Committee's resource, which is titled *The Student Evaluation Standards: How to Improve Evaluations of Students*. It is, quite literally, *the* source for the student evaluation standards; and it is also quite easy to read, understand, and use. In addition to presenting and describing the standards, *The Student Evaluation Standards* provides a wealth of guidelines and case examples that help illustrate the standards in practical terms. For our purposes, however, it is sufficient to provide an overview of the Student Evaluation Standards, which are intended to guide and govern student assessment and evaluation that may occur in any context, be it high-stakes state standardized assessments, psychometrically designed diagnostic tests, or a third-grade teacher's weekly vocabulary quiz. Let's take a brief look at each of these four attributes from the vantage point of the classroom teacher.

First, the **propriety standards** remind us that when we assess students, we must do so in ways that protect students from any undue harm. This means, foremost, that our classroom-based assessments should directly serve the educational needs of students and, therefore, serve to promote student learning. Attention to propriety also means that we should employ classroom assessments equitably with our students and that we should protect students' confidentiality, therefore sharing and using assessment information only with individuals with legitimate interests in and responsibilities for a student's learning (e.g., school leaders, counselors, other teachers, and, of course, parents and guardians). The propriety standards also remind us that the processes of assessment and evaluation should be respectful of students—not demeaning or deliberately discouraging—and that these processes should not harm students' general welfare and health. Also, when we attend to propriety as teachers, we understand that assessment should be balanced in its emphasis on weaknesses to be addressed in students' learning as well as strengths on which to build. Finally, the propriety standards require that we be conscious of our own potential conflicts of interest—for example, those times when our own roles as family members, friends, or subordinates may influence our judgments and decision making. In such instances, we must be open and honest in identifying and resolving potential conflicts. In short, the propriety standards require that teacher-made, classroom-based assessments be legal, fair, and do no harm to students.

Next, the **utility standards** remind us as teachers that our classroom-based assessments must be purposeful and practical. Most importantly, the utility standards require that assessments should lead to decision making that ultimately contributes to and supports ongoing student learning. Related to such decision making, classroom assessments should clearly identify *who* is involved in the assessment and evaluation processes, as well as identify the type and amount of information that these processes are intended to produce. Also, as we suggested in Chapter 1, teachers must have the requisite knowledge and skills to construct, conduct, and use assessments appropriately in their classrooms, which includes being aware of and articulating the values by which judgments and decisions about student learning are rendered. Finally, the utility standards require that assessment in the classroom should lead to timely, accurate, and relevant communication with students, parents, and other educators; furthermore, they should result in practical follow-up on judgments and decision making in ways that support ongoing student learning. In summary, the utility standards require that teacher-made assessments have practical use in the classroom that supports student learning.

Third, the **feasibility standards** remind us that our teacher-made assessments must be doable. For example, if an assessment in the classroom becomes so time-consuming or so disruptive that student learning is diminished or if an assessment is so elaborate or resource-intensive that the teacher simply cannot pull it off within the context of the classroom, the assessment violates the feasibility standards. More specifically, the feasibility standards require that teacher-made assessments efficiently and effectively use time and resources, so as not to take away from teaching and learning. The feasibility standards also remind us that communication is inherent to the processes of assessment and evaluation; therefore, teachers must be attentive to the viability of communicating assessment results, judgments, and decision making to others, such as students, parents, and fellow educators. In short, the feasibility standards require that teacher-made assessments be realistic in their intent and design, so that they can, in fact, be used in actual classroom settings.

Finally, the **accuracy standards** remind us as teachers that we must assess students to adequately and dependably represent student learning, so we can make decisions that ultimately support further learning. This means that teachers must be clear about what knowledge and skills are being assessed and about the expected level of achievement or performance. This constitutes the criteria by which student learning is assessed. The accuracy standards also require that teachers identify and consider situational factors that may influence student performance; and teachers must identify the means of accounting for, if not mitigating, such influences so that students have opportunities to demonstrate the truest nature and degree of their learning. This effort includes the need for teachers to be aware of and account for their own biases, as well as biases that may be present in commercially or institutionally produced materials they use. The accuracy standards also address the need to attend to the appropriate use of assessment results when rendering judgments and making decisions about student learning. Teachers must review assessment results purposefully and systematically to use them to support ongoing student learning. This includes considering how to most effectively and constructively provide and employ feedback to students and others. The intent throughout the accuracy standards is that judgments and decision making be justifiable and meaningful to teachers as well as others in the educational process. Finally, the accuracy standards direct teachers to be ever mindful of the attributes of good assessments and to be attentive to ways to improve their classroom-based assessments to serve the larger aim of ongoing student learning. In summary, the accuracy standards require that teacher-made assessments provide appropriate and dependable information about student learning to facilitate the education process.

Validity and Reliability: The Core Principles of Good Assessment Practices

The Student Evaluation Standards provide an essential and comprehensive overview of the attributes of an effective and appropriate assessment. Although the attributes of propriety, utility, and feasibility are important in their own right, the attribute of accuracy includes two principles that are at the core of good assessment, namely, *validity* and *reliability*. Figure 2.2 illustrates the role of validity and reliability in relation to the Student Evaluation Standards. In the figure, the four attributes of the standards together comprise what we have rather casually described as "A Really Good Test!" The point is, of course, that a good assessment is characterized by qualities of propriety, utility, feasibility, and accuracy. But Figure 2.2 is also intended to illustrate the relative importance of validity and reliability as *core principles* of good assessment practices. Validity and reliability are central to and also largely comprise the accuracy standards. Referring to the Student Evaluation Standards presented in the Appendix, the principles of validity and reliability constitute the first seven of the 12 accuracy standards; or, seen another way, the principles of validity and reliability constitute fully one-fourth of the 28 total standards. Although the sheer number of standards suggests the central importance of validity and reliability, the centrality of these principles is evident conceptually as well. Namely, if an assessment is *not* valid and reliable, it is inherently unfair, impractical, worthless, and inaccurate. In other words, without validity and reliability, the Student Evaluation Standards of propriety, utility, feasibility, and accuracy are lost.

So, we turn our attention to the two core assessment principles of validity and reliability.

Figure 2.2. Validity and Reliability as Core Principles of the Student Evaluation Standards

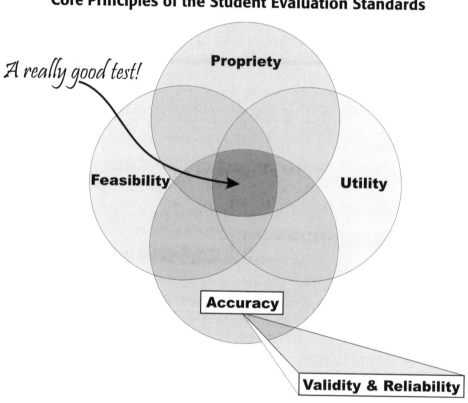

Validity and Reliability in Everyday Life

People use the terms *valid* and *reliable* all the time, and not just in educational settings. For example, an informal conversation between friends debating the merits of a local politician's tax proposal leads to one of the friends responding to the other, "You can't say that. Your point's just not *valid!*" A woman at the counter of the cell phone kiosk says to the salesclerk, "I'm not happy with my phone. I never know when I'll have reception and when I won't. It's just not *reliable.*" In common, everyday situations like these, the terms *valid* and *reliable* have generally understood meanings. Consider this:

◆ When we say *valid*, we're likely to mean *truthful, suitable, legitimate, applicable, convincing, compelling.*

◆ When we say *reliable*, we're likely to mean *dependable, consistent, stable, error-free.*

To explore this idea further, we asked a group of veteran teachers to tell us about situations in their own experiences in which the concepts of validity and reliability were at play. But, as a catch, we asked them about situations from *everyday life*—that is, their experiences outside of the classroom. Three of these are presented in the following boxes called Teacher-to-Teacher. As you read, keep in mind that this is a fellow teacher *talking* to you in her or his own voice.

TEACHER-TO-TEACHER

Reliability in Everyday Life—*Strep Test*

A recent experience my son and I had illustrates the concept of reliability and its relationship to **inferences** that may follow a test. In this case, it was a medical test—the rapid strep throat test used to diagnose the presence of strep throat infection. Is the rapid strep throat test a **reliable** way to accurately diagnose the presence of the streptococcal bacteria on the throat? Well, only sort of. As many as 33% of the tests completed report a negative result when the streptococcal bacteria is actually present in the throat. Due to the **unreliability** of the rapid strep test, a throat culture often follows a negative result to ensure a **reliable** diagnosis. So, the rapid strep throat test is adequate for making an initial diagnosis in a clinic, but it is not **dependable** enough to draw a conclusive diagnosis.

Ann
Elementary Teacher

TEACHER-TO-TEACHER
Validity in Everyday Life—*American Idol*

On the television show *American Idol*, each week millions of viewers assess the performances of a variety of singers and vote to determine the next pop artist. The contestants are challenged to sing different songs from different genres. Critiques from the show's judges who work in the entertainment industry may or may not influence the votes of the viewing public. It is **inferred** that the winner of the competition will become a successful entertainer. Because performers are sometimes asked to sing songs that are not suitable for their voices or they may not have the charisma of others, they may lose favor with the audience and not earn enough votes to keep them in the competition. Some voters may rally for the "underdog" or who they perceive as the least talented competitor. When this happens, the assessment no longer is a **true measure** of vocal talent, stage presence, and other attributes that ensure success in the entertainment industry. There is also no information about how the opinions of the voters represent the overall American public. These factors question the **validity** of the competition's results. Although many former contestants, some of whom were not the winners of the competition, have been successful when tested in the real world of entertainment, few have achieved the true status of *American Idol*, so the competition has only limited **predictive value**.

Karen
Middle School Teacher

TEACHER-TO-TEACHER
Reliability in Everyday Life—*Referees*

As a coach, player, and avid sports fan, I appreciate **reliability** on the field of play within the realm of athletics. In this situation, **reliability** relates to the officials. Most people don't like to say they won or lost because of the officiating, but all would agree they look for **consistency** from their officials. Both teams want an even opportunity to compete and win, and they hold the officials accountable to call the game in a fair manner. While most home teams rely on the officials for a few calls, I believe most would agree that they would prefer a fair game as opposed to one won with controversy. A game in which the rules of the sport are applied **consistently** is a fair game. This is **reliable** officiating.

Nate
High School Teacher

Validity and Reliability of Teacher-Made Tests

The concepts of validity and reliability function in the realm of teacher-made assessments essentially in the same way as they function in the *everyday life* scenarios just presented. In short, validity is concerned with the truthfulness or appropriateness of decisions resulting from assessments, and reliability is concerned with the dependability or stability of those results. One common means of visually depicting these concepts is by thinking of validity as an archery target and thinking of reliability as the results of shots at the target. This is visually presented in Figure 2.3.

Figure 2.3. A Visual Depiction of Validity and Reliability

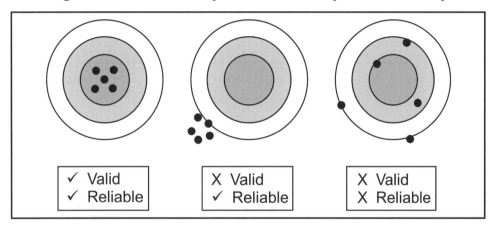

The first picture in Figure 2.3 is a visual metaphor of a valid and reliable assessment. The intended target—the bull's eye in the center of the circular target—is struck shot after shot. In short, this suggests that the correct target is being aimed at and the target is being hit consistently. Thus, validity and reliability are evident.

In the second picture in Figure 2.3, the shots land consistently at a particular location. Thus, the shots are reliable. However, the shots are off target. This illustrates an assessment that is invalid—it is simply aimed at the wrong thing!

The third picture presents another possible scenario. In this case, the shots are aimed at the target; however, they are striking the target in an unpredictable array of locations. In other words, the shots are landing in an unreliable pattern. In this picture, therefore, the unreliable pattern of shots—some of which hit the target and others do not—prevents any consistent inferences about performance. In other words, the lack of reliability detracts from the validity.

These illustrations can be quite helpful in thinking about the concepts of validity and reliability. However, as with any metaphor, the visual metaphors in Figure 2.3 present an important, but limited, understanding of validity and reliability. There are other attributes of these concepts that teachers, as professionals, should understand. In the following sections, therefore, we explore the characteristics of validity and reliability, as well as some practical means of ensuring their presence for teacher-made assessments. We conclude by then looking at how validity and reliability interact with and influence each other.

Validity

The attribute of validity is arguably the most important quality of an assessment.[5] As suggested by the examples presented in the prior section, validity is concerned with the appropriateness or meaningfulness of an assessment's target. In other words, validity is concerned with whether a test, quiz, project, or performance assesses what we intend it to assess. However, inherent in this understanding of validity is the supposition that validity hinges on someone rendering *judgments*, making *decisions*, or drawing *inferences* based on results of an assessment.[6] Thus, a more accurate definition of **validity** is the extent to which inferences drawn from assessment results are appropriate.

Typically, when we talk about the validity of a test, we do not do so in absolute terms. Rarely is a test either perfectly valid or perfectly invalid. Validity is usually a question of degree. Indeed, we would even argue that no assessment is inherently valid, because assessments are, by design, samplings of intended behavior under fixed or simulated conditions and, therefore, are never truly and completely authentic. The point that classroom teachers should keep in mind is that no test, however well conceived and constructed, is perfectly valid.

Again, validity is a matter of degree. Therefore, when contemplating and discussing the validity of an assessment, it is best to use relative terms, such as *high validity, moderate validity,* and *low validity.* For example, rather than saying, "My unit test is valid," you might say, "My unit test has a high degree of validity," thereby accounting for the diminished validity inherent in any assessment. Perhaps you administer a social studies quiz from a commercially produced textbook series. Your intent is to use the results to gauge the degree of student learning so far in the unit, but you are well aware that the quiz requires a good deal of reading. You also know that a portion of your class is one or more grade levels behind in their reading comprehension skills. You may say that the test has "moderate validity for my lower-level reading students." In this situation, the quiz may have a high degree of validity in assessing social studies content from the unit, but the influence of reading comprehension on the ability of some of your students to demonstrate their knowledge from the unit limits the *inferences* you can draw about their learning in social studies. Thus, the validity of the quiz is reduced somewhat.

To review, validity is concerned with the confidence with which we may draw inferences about student learning from an assessment. Furthermore, validity is not an either/or proposition; instead, it is a matter of degree.

A third important idea regarding validity that teachers should understand is that validity is a *unified concept,* consisting of four attributes that together comprise the notion of validity. A helpful analogy is to liken validity to a diamond gemstone. A diamond is a beautiful creation of nature. A diamond is also an expensive commodity! How do jewelers decide how to place value on (that is, put a price tag on) a diamond? They consider the four Cs: cut, color, carat weight, and clarity. Similarly, when we consider the validity of an assessment, we can also consider four Cs; although the Cs stand for different concepts than they do for diamonds. When we consider validity, we contemplate evidence related to *construct, content, criterion,* and *consequential* validity.

You might even consider these components of validity as being like the *facets* of a diamond, as represented in Figure 2.4. A diamond is a single gemstone; however, it is comprised of multiple faces or facets that interact with each other and with light to create the visual presence for which diamonds are so valued. The attribute of validity as related to a classroom-based assessment is similar. The validity of the assessment is a function of the multiple facets of the four types of validity evidence, each contributing to the overall degree of validity.

Figure 2.4. Four Facets of Validity

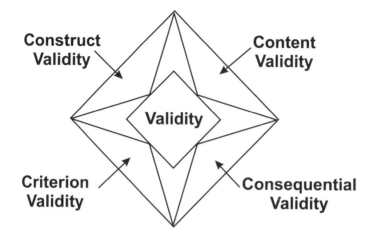

So, understanding that validity is a single concept comprised of four facets, how do you then gauge the validity of an assessment? As alluded to previously, you look for and consider *evidence* of each of the various types of validity. In the next several sections, we describe each of the four facets of validity and ways of gauging the degree of each.

Construct Validity

Construct-related evidence of validity is concerned with how accurately an assessment aligns with the theoretical framework of the intended learning outcomes, standards, or objectives of the instructional unit. In other words, construct validity asks, "Does the assessment measure what it purports to measure?" Returning to the archery analogy from earlier, construct validity asks, "Are we shooting at the proper target?" When considered in these terms, it is easy to see why construct validity is usually considered the most fundamental and encompassing of the four types of validity.[7]

Construct validity is at once simple and complex to gauge. For example, construct validity is also known as **face validity,** which has been defined as "the *appearance* of validity."[8] Thus, to gauge the construct validity of a test, you could simply consider whether the test "would *look* valid and be acceptable to the test taker and to the public generally."[9] This criterion brings to mind the old quip that if a bird looks like a duck, walks like a duck, and quacks like a duck, then it must be a duck. If a test has math on it and students have to do math to complete it, then it must be a math test.

But it is at this point that the concept of construct validity becomes more complicated, because math is a complex discipline made up of myriad points of facts, principles, skills, and applications. A test, quiz, project, or other assessment—even at the highest levels of study—is going to target a limited scope of standards or objectives related to the mathematics that a teacher and her students are currently studying. Therefore, to gauge the construct validity of the assessment, you need to know the specific learning objectives of the unit of study. In other words, you would need to know what content students were intended to learn and the cognitive level at which they were to engage with the content. Now, if you happen to have subject-area expertise in mathematics, a list of such objectives may make perfect sense to you. But, if you happen to be an English teacher, it may be difficult for you to confidently determine the construct validity of the assessment, because you may not have the depth of subject-area knowledge needed. This is a practical reality, and it is important to realize: At face value, assessments may appear valid; however, to accurately judge the construct validity of a quiz, test, project, essay, or other assessment, you must have a depth of expertise in the subject area itself.

Content Validity

Content-related evidence of validity is concerned with how adequately an assessment samples the intended learning outcomes, standards, or objectives of an instructional unit. Assessments, by definition, are intended to be representative of the assessment taker's knowledge and/or skills in a particular set of standards or objectives.[10] This is because of the fact that assessments are typically limited by the time and resources available for the act of assessing.[11] Thus, an assessment samples from among a set of learning objectives, creating an incomplete but hopefully representative picture of a student's learning. Indeed, content validity is sometimes referred to as *sampling validity*.

Content validity, then, is concerned with ensuring that an assessment adequately samples the standards or objectives of an instructional unit and, conversely, that it does *not* assess learning outcomes that were not intended for nor taught to students. Thus, gauging the content validity of an assessment begins much the way gauging construct validity begins: You must first know the learning objectives of the instructional unit. From here, you then create a **table of specifications** to account for each of the learning objectives, as well as to ensure that extraneous learning objectives are not unintentionally assessed. We explain the creation of a table of specifications in detail in Chapter 3. Suffice it to say here, however, that creating a table of specifications requires a degree of professional knowledge and technical skill of teachers. However, in our experiences as teachers, teacher-leaders, and instructional supervisors, many current teachers are simply unaware of what a table of specifications is or how to create one whether for a unit test, an extended project, or a short quiz. Yet, creating a table of specifications is one of the most practical, essential, and easy steps by which to construct a valid assessment. Again, we address this competency in detail in the next chapter, but Figure 2.5 summarizes a study that illustrates the unintended negative consequences when content validity is weakened.

Figure 2.5. Summary of a Study of the Content Validity of Teacher-Made Math Tests

Are Teachers Testing Higher Order Thinking?[12]

In a study of teacher-made tests in grades K–12 across core subject areas, researchers analyzed individual test items to determine the cognitive level required to respond to each question. They found that 72% of test items functioned at the knowledge level, 11% at the comprehension level, 15% at the application level, 1% at the analysis level, and less than 1% at either the synthesis or evaluation level. Nearly half of the 28% of questions that functioned beyond the knowledge level were on math tests, on which computational (i.e., application) problems are more prevalent. Notably, almost 98% of items on social studies tests were at the knowledge level.

How are these findings related to validity? Validity concerns whether the inferences drawn from test results are appropriate. If a student scores 100% on a typical social studies test from this sample, what can we infer about her learning? Can we infer, for example, her ability to interpret historical events and relate historical lessons to contemporary experiences? Given that 98% of the test assesses at the knowledge level, we cannot draw such inferences. However, if the teacher, student, parent, and next year's teacher all are under the impression that the student's grade on the test is indicative of historical interpretation and critical thinking, the inferences they each draw about the student's learning are simply inappropriate. In other words, the inferences from the test have a *low degree of validity*.

Criterion Validity

Criterion-related evidence of validity is concerned with how accurately an assessment equates with another assessment that is intended to measure the same learning outcomes, standards, or objectives. Criterion validity can be determined when two related assessments occur in proximity to each other. If two assessments presume to measure the same learning outcomes and do so within a common period of time, the results on the two assessments are indicative of **concurrent validity.** If two assessments measure the same learning outcomes but do so at distinctly different points in time, determining whether the first assessment predicts performance on the second assessment is indicative of **predictive validity.**

As an example of concurrent validity, consider Virginia's current accountability system, which is similar in design to several other state systems. In Virginia, high school students are required to pass state assessments of the Standards of Learning (SOL) for certain core courses in mathematics, English, history, and science. These assessments are called *end-of-course tests,* and they must be passed for a student to receive credit for designated courses. In this case, two assessments are occurring concurrently to measure student learning: The student earns a grade in the course and the student also earns a grade on the end-of-course SOL test. Both the course grade and the end-of-course test grade are intended to indicate proficiency in the same set of state curriculum standards and at essentially the same time (i.e., at or near the end of study in the course). Presumably, therefore, students who pass the course will also pass the end-of-course test. Indeed, such is the faith in the concurrent validity of the SOL end-of-course tests that if a student passes his course but does *not* pass the related test, he doesn't receive credit for the course. In this scenario a teacher may question the validity of one or the other of the assessments because the assessments are intended to measure the same learning outcomes, but the different results lead to conflicting inferences. The teacher would need to turn to evidence of content validity (as indicated by tables of specifications of the respective assessments) and to evidence of construct validity (by reviewing the appropriateness of the learning objectives on which the assessments are based) to gauge the relative validity of the assessments. Of course, what complicates the concurrent validity of comparing classroom grades to standardized assessment results is that classroom grades presumably assess learning objectives *beyond* the objectives assessed by standardized assessments. Oftentimes, grades include assessments of knowledge and skills demonstrated best through projects, labs, and participation—elements of learning that standardized tests cannot and do not attempt to tap. Thus, the estimation of concurrent validity becomes quite limited.

As for predictive validity, it functions in the same way as in the previous example, with the exception that the two assessments in question occur at distinctly different points in time. For example, the same teacher in Virginia may give her students a practice end-of-course test in the weeks prior to the actual test to predict students' performance on the high-stakes assessment and to plan for further targeted instruction. In this scenario the teacher would gauge the *predictive validity* by reviewing individual students' results on the practice test and comparing those results to performance on the end-of-course test. The more consistent individual students' scores between the two tests, the stronger the evidence of predictive validity. The farther apart the actual results from the expected results, the weaker the evidence—and the need to look to *content* and *construct* validity.

Consequential Validity

Consequential-related evidence of validity is concerned with the appropriateness of the intended and unintended outcomes that ensue from an assessment. Such outcomes can include entry into programs or services, such as honor societies, advanced courses, remediation services, or special education services. They can also include promotion to the next grade level, graduation from high school, and admission into postsecondary education. Outcomes can also be affective in nature, influencing student motivation, beliefs, or dispositions.

For example, a struggling student may perform well on an assessment in preparation for which the teacher had scaffolded learning and which the student judged to be a fair test of her learning. The consequence may be a more positive attitude toward the teacher, the subject, and learning, more generally. In this example, the consequence is positive and ultimately leads to improving student learning. The teacher may conclude, therefore, that the test has a high degree of consequential validity for this particular student regarding her sense of self-efficacy for learning. Conversely, the consequences of an assessment may be more insidious. If an assessment is perceived to be unfairly difficult, to assess knowledge or skills that were inadequately taught, or to be administered in such a way that students are unable to demonstrate their true learning, negative perceptions and feelings may be engendered. If in such a situation the teacher had aimed, in part, to foster not only knowledge of but also an appreciation for the scientific method in his students, the assessment may diminish its very validity because the test itself inadvertently hinders students' acquisition of this important intended outcome of learning.

Assessment results—and the inferences that follow—can have profound effects. Some of these effects are intentional and deliberate; others are unexpected and perhaps even unnoticed. Some are productive and affirming; others are insidious and destructive. As is evident from the previous examples, consequential validity can potentially play a significant role in teaching and learning. However, consequential validity is sometimes overlooked. Perhaps this is because the three other types of validity evidence—construct, content, and criterion validity—are more technical in nature and can be more readily observed. Whatever the case, consequential validity plays a centrally vital role in teaching and learning. Simply put, teachers must come to consider their assessment practices as integral to their instructional practices. And, just as most teachers recognize that positive regard, engagement, and relevancy are doorways to student learning, so too must teachers realize that their assessment practices should be engaging, fair, and relevant, as well. Rick Stiggins, a noted author and presenter in the area of classroom assessment, puts it this way:

> Assessment practices that permit, even encourage, some students to give up on learning must be replaced by those that engender hope and sustained effort for all students. In short, the entire emotional environment surrounding the experience of being evaluated must change for all, but especially for perennial low achievers.[13]

Tips for Gauging Validity

Validity is a single, unified concept, comprised of four essential facets. Figure 2.6 explores each of these four distinguishing features, and provides some practical questions and evidence that would help teachers to gauge the validity of assessments used in the classroom.

Reliability

Closely related to the concept of *validity* is the concept of *reliability*. In fact, the two concepts of assessment are integrally related and together constitute the core principles of good assessment. So, what is reliability? **Reliability** is the consistency or dependability of the results of an assessment.

Central to the principle of reliability is the relative absence of error. First, let's consider what error in an assessment is. **Error** in an assessment is when an assessment item does not adequately distinguish between the student who has truly mastered the intended learning outcome and the student who has not. For example, when a student gets a question correct, not because she knows it but because of something other than knowledge of or skill in the intended learning being assessed, assessment error has occurred. Similarly, if a student misses a question for some reason other than a lack of knowledge or skill, then error has occurred.

As with validity, reliability is a matter of degree. Rarely is a single test question or an assessment perfectly reliable. Rather, a test item or a comprehensive assessment may be relatively free of error, or, put differently, it may be more or less reliable. The fact is that *no* assessment is free of error. Every test has some degree of error. This fact becomes more evident when you consider that there are essentially two types of error to which all assessments are subject: *systematic error* and *random error*. Figure 2.7 depicts these two types of error. In the figure, systematic error is represented by the

Figure 2.6. Facets of Validity: Questions to Ask and Evidence to Gather

Facets of Validity	Questions a Teacher Can Ask to Gauge Validity	Evidence a Teacher Can Gather to Determine Validity
Construct related	• Can we infer a student's knowledge and/or skills in this subject area from the assessment?	• Unpack the intended learning outcomes, standards, and/or objectives that the assessment is intended to tap to determine their appropriateness for the curricular goals of this unit of instruction (see Chapter 3). • Create a table of specifications and review its adequacy in representing the intended learning outcomes of the instructional unit (see Chapter 3).
Content related	• Does the assessment adequately sample the intended learning outcomes? • Are there items on the assessment with no corresponding intended learning outcomes?	• Create a table of specifications and review it to ensure that the assessment adequately samples the intended learning outcomes and does not inadvertently assess learning outcomes that were not intended (see Chapter 3).
Criterion related	• Does the assessment measure intended outcomes of learning that are also measured on some other assessment? • Concurrent evidence: Can we estimate performance on a related assessment completed within the same time frame based on performance on the present assessment? • Predictive evidence: Can the assessment predict performance on a future assessment purported to measure the same learning objectives?	• Compare performance on a current test that purports to assess related intended learning outcomes (e.g., state assessments or Advanced Placement exams). • Compare performance on a future assessment purported to assess related learning outcomes (e.g., college-entrance tests or grade point averages in college).
Consequential related	• What are the consequences of using the assessment for decision making regarding student learning? For better or worse, are there any unintended consequences of this assessment for students?	Identify and judge the appropriateness of effects on: • Student motivation, attitudes, beliefs, etc. • Placement in and/or access to special designations or programs • Instructional decisions • Inferences drawn from parents, other educators, etc.

small sphere, suggesting that sources of systematic tend to be relatively limited and, when looked for, detectable. Random error, however, can be caused by any number of situations and is not always knowable or even detectable; therefore, random error in the figure is represented by the vast space around the sphere of systematic error.

Figure 2.7. Types of Error

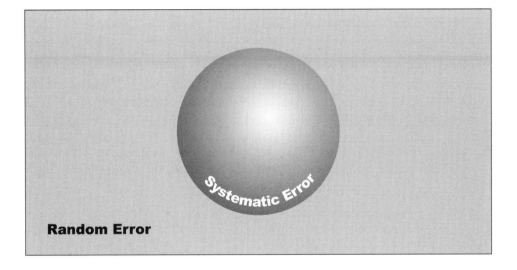

Systematic error is error that is unintentionally built into an assessment but may be controlled when detected. Examples of systematic error include the following:

- ◆ Culturally biased language and expressions
- ◆ Developmentally inappropriate reading level
- ◆ Mechanical or grammatical mistakes in assessment items
- ◆ Insufficient or unclear directions
- ◆ Poor layout of the assessment, causing uncertainty or mistakes in reading the assessment
- ◆ Insufficient number of assessment items
- ◆ Subjective scoring
- ◆ Cheating

Random error is error that influences assessment results but is not controllable. As suggested by Figure 2.7, the possible sources of random error are essentially limitless, but some common examples include the following, just to name a few:

- Illness
- Carelessness
- Luck (or unluckiness!)
- Unhappiness
- Momentary distractedness
- Giddiness
- Fire alarm
- Intercom announcement
- Wobbly desk

Imagine, for example, a straight-A, ninth-grade student whose day takes a turn for the worse. He walks into his third-period history class expecting to take the test he has dutifully studied for the past three nights in a row. The problem is, in the hallway he just found out that the girl he was going to ask to the homecoming dance just said yes to some tenth grader. Our ninth grader is a bit upset but also embarrassed, because this is the first dance at his new school and he doesn't have any other prospects. He's already racking his brain trying to figure out who else he could ask; and, at the same time, he's trying to decide how to play this off with his buddies at the lunch table during fourth period. They're sure to find out, and they are just as sure to razz him about it. Then he sits down at his desk. There's gum in the chair. Not too fresh, but fresh enough to stick to his pants. Should he try to peel it off? or should he be nonchalant—as nonchalant as you can be with bright pink bubble gum on your tail side. His history teacher, in the meantime, passes around the test and immediately launches into giving oral directions for how to complete the test. Our straight-A student is about to experience *error* on this assessment of his learning. He misses key directions from the teacher, and experiences *systematic error* because of the teacher's oral directions. This could have been controlled if the teacher had more deliberately facilitated the students' transition into the class and, specifically, into the testing situation. Providing the directions in writing for students to refer to as she spoke would have helped, too; but she was up late last night writing the test, as it was. Of course, the student also experiences *random error*. Through no fault of his or of the teacher's (blame the dastardly tenth grader), the student's frame of mind for taking this test has been clouded. He may pull himself together and be able to concentrate; but chances are that his distracted emotional state may cause him to, quite literally, make an error or two in his responses . . . or worse. In short, this student's results on this particular assessment may not be a completely reliable indication of what he actually knows about this unit of study in his ninth-grade history class. Under different circumstances, he would likely perform better.

The fact is, such scenarios—and a myriad of other ones—play out every single day in schools. But we don't mean to be melodramatic. Nor are we suggesting that it's incumbent on the teacher to psychoanalyze each student prior to a quiz or test to account for the slings and arrows suffered in the course of normal human interactivity. Instead, our intent is to reduce the *hubris* with which we, as teachers, sometimes treat assessment in our classrooms. Assessment is an imperfect art; every assessment is subject to unintended error. We, as teachers, simply need to be reminded of this.

Reliability is concerned with whether the results of a student's performance on an assessment are a true indication of the student's learning, and not results unduly influenced by error. Because of the importance of reliability in interpreting assessment results, psychometricians (that is, people who construct and study assessments for a living) have developed a number of tools for understanding the influence of error on assessments. Through *item analysis* procedures, for example, one can compute *reliability coefficients* on a scale of 0 to 1 that indicate the degree of score stability of an assessment. An assessment can be analyzed to determine the *standard error of measure,* which represents the difference between a student's achieved score and her theoretical *true score.* These and other concepts are especially important when reviewing, analyzing, discussing, and making decisions based on high-stakes assessments. Frankly, however, they are less critical to the typical classroom teacher who is mainly concerned with constructing and using reasonably valid and reliable assessments of student learning.

Tips for Ensuring Reliability

How, then, can a classroom teacher try to ensure the reliability of his or her classroom-based assessments? Essentially, there are three ways, which are summarized in Figure 2.8.

Figure 2.8. Ensuring the Reliability of an Assessment

Questions a Teacher Can Ask to Gauge Reliability	Steps a Teacher Can Take to Improve Reliability
Do I have enough questions for each core objective or intended learning that I am assessing?	As a general rule, include three or more test questions or items for each core objective to reduce the unintended effects of error on the assessment results.
Are the questions, directions, and formatting on the assessment free from systematic error?	Review and proofread individual test questions, prompts, and directions for systematic error, including grammatical or mechanical mistakes, cultural biases, lack of clarity, etc.
Are the criteria for grading the assessment as objective as possible?	Clarify and verify grading criteria for the test, including rubrics. Ensure intra-rater and inter-rater reliability by establishing scoring protocols and training.

First, the teacher should ask, "Do I have a sufficient number of assessment items for each outcome of learning I intend to measure from this unit of study?" As a general rule of test construction, the more items to which students respond, the more reliable the instrument. Let's say a fourth-grade math teacher is giving a test on adding and subtracting decimals. If she puts only one addition problem on the test and one subtraction problem, then how confident can she be in a student's results? If a student misses one out of one addition questions, should the teacher assume the student knows nothing about adding decimals? To account for the possibility of error—that is, to account for the possibility that a student may miss a question for reasons unrelated to knowledge or skills—the fourth-grade teacher would be wise to include several addition problems and several subtraction problems. Then, if a student misses all of the addition problems, the teacher can be reasonably confident that the student does not understand how to add decimals. Similarly, if a student gets all the addition problems correct, the teacher could have a relatively high degree of confidence in the stability of the student's performance—that is, the teacher could reliably infer that the student knows how to add decimals.

Of course, a teacher must decide *how many* questions is enough to ensure reliability. Although there are no set rules to guide teachers, some common sense is helpful. Minimally, a teacher would want to *triangulate* each core objective of study. Thus, three questions for each main topic of knowledge or specific skill application offers a reasonable guideline from which to begin. However, more than three questions asked about a specific objective serves to improve reliability still more, because the teacher then has a greater number of responses from each student to establish a pattern of demonstrated learning or lack thereof.

But there is an upper limit to how many questions should be asked on an assessment. Again, no specific number is the rule; rather, a teacher must be aware of the length of assessment that is reasonable for the age of students in the class. After all, if, in your quest for greater reliability, you ask too many questions, you could unintentionally *decrease* reliability by introducing weariness into the testing situation, which could lead to error. With this caveat firmly in mind, the general guideline for a teacher to remember is, to improve the reliability of an assessment, be sure to include an adequate number of items on the assessment for each core learning objective. Typically, the more questions asked for each learning objective, the better able the teacher is to gauge the reliability of results.

A second question a teacher should ask to gauge reliability is, "Are the questions, directions, and formatting on the assessment free from systematic error?" Error can be introduced to an assessment in a variety of ways. If a test question is poorly worded, a student may misinterpret the question and, therefore, answer it incorrectly because of the wording, not because of his degree of learning. If directions for a project are unclear or are unintentionally incomplete, a student who may otherwise perform well on the assignment may miss a critical element. If a multiple choice item requires students to use a map on one page to answer questions stapled to subsequent pages that follow, the very act of flipping back and forth between pages may introduce error. If information in question #3 on a quiz unintentionally provides the answer to #6 on the quiz, the student who does *not* possess the knowledge to answer #6 under different circumstances may get it correct.

With each of these examples, the chain of events is the same: Something in the construction of the assessment itself unintentionally causes a student either to get the question wrong when she actually possesses the assessed learning or to get the question correct when she actually does not possess the assessed learning. In these examples, the source of the error can usually be detected through careful proofreading, which suggests these instances describe *systematic error*: error that, while unintentional, can be identified and controlled.

Even in an age of the ubiquitous spell checker and even in a time when commercially produced test banks accompany many textbook series, the introduction of such error is quite common. In our own experiences reviewing teacher-made assessments, we come across such problems quite frequently. Why do such errors in the construction of assessments occur? We have identified three main reasons:

1. Sometimes teachers and commercial test producers do not proofread their assessments carefully for common grammatical and mechanical errors.

2. Sometimes teachers and commercial test producers do not know and follow the guidelines for constructing certain types of assessment items (which we present and review in Chapters 4 and 5).

3. Sometimes teachers and commercial test producers make incorrect assumptions about students' prior learning, background knowledge, and reading abilities.

How, then, can you as a teacher attempt to ensure against these and thereby improve the reliability of your assessments? Here are a few suggestions:

◆ Use your spell checker.

◆ Have a colleague proofread your assessment for clarity and correctness.

◆ Review and follow the guidelines for constructing different item types, such as multiple choice, true-false, short answer, and essay questions.

◆ Consciously consider the cultural and academic backgrounds of your students as you write individual items.

◆ Consciously examine your own cultural background and assumptions.

◆ Be aware of conditions during assessment that may interfere with students' ability to focus and sustain effort.

A third question a teacher can ask to gauge the reliability of an assessment is, "Are the criteria for grading the assessment as objective as possible?" Not only can error be inadvertently built into an assessment when the teacher is creating it, but error can also occur when an assessment is being scored. It could be something as simple as an answer key being incorrect and, therefore, students systematically getting question #15 marked incorrect, when, in fact, their answers are correct. Error in grading also occurs when scoring is so subjective that a student's score comes to depend on factors such as where in the stack his paper was graded or the teacher's mood when grading rather than depending on meeting the criteria of an appropriate response. Written responses such as short answers and essays are especially subject to this, but it can also be the case with a math teacher subjectively awarding partial credit for computation responses, a choir teacher grading a student's performance, or an art teacher assessing a student's clay project.

To control error in the grading process, a teacher should aim to reduce subjectivity as much as possible and to increase the likelihood that a student's score on an assessment would be the same regardless of when it was graded, what order it was graded in, or under what circumstances it was graded. This principle of assessment is called **intra-rater reliability;** and it means that a scorer consistently applies the scoring criteria to an assessment thereby resulting in a stable score, uninfluenced by factors that are not the criteria of learning. In other words, the teacher grades each paper as fairly and objectively as possible. The same principle applies if two or more teachers have co-created an assessment for their students and the consistent application of the scoring criteria by each of the teachers results in accurate scores among students, regardless of which teacher grades which student's work. This is called **inter-rater reliability.**

Appropriately applying criteria when scoring assessments is a critical step in ensuring reliability. This is especially true when using student-created responses, such as computational problems, short answers, essays, projects, performances, and original creations. Such items require a teacher to identify the expected criteria of performance and to determine gradations or levels of possible student work. Techniques for scoring student-supplied responses include *checklists, rating scales,* and *rubrics.* We explore these techniques in Chapter 5.

What Does It Mean to Have a Valid and Reliable Test?

If an assessment allows you to draw inferences about the nature and degree of student learning regarding a known set of standards or objectives, and if the assessment also allows you to distinguish between the student who has truly acquired those standards or objectives and the student who has not, then you have a valid and reliable assessment.

If the assessment inadvertently measures a different set of objectives, inadequately measures the various components that make up the intended objectives, fails to predict performance on another assessment that measures the same objectives, or unintentionally infringes on a student's acquisition of the intended objectives, then the validity of the assessment is diminished.

If the assessment inadvertently allows a student's results to suggest acquisition of the intended objectives when, in fact, they have not been acquired or inadvertently allows a student's results to suggest a *lack* of acquisition of the objectives when, in fact, the objectives have been acquired, then the reliability of the assessment is diminished.

With the preceding summations of validity and reliability in mind, we conclude our overview of these core principles of assessment by considering several examples. We asked a group of experienced teachers to describe a situation from their own teaching practice that illustrated the principles of validity and reliability in play. The examples come from elementary, middle, and high school settings, as well as from a variety of subject areas. In each case the teacher shares the application of the concepts of validity and reliability with us in his or her own words. What's more, in each case the teacher critiques his or her past practice with regard to creating and/or using valid and reliable assessments in the classroom.

TEACHER-TO-TEACHER
Validity and Reliability With My Students

As educators, I'm sure that we could all fill pages about our experiences with **unreliable** or **invalid** assessments. For example, in my current school, teachers must use Cloze tests to determine the reading level of students. Cloze tests are assessments in which students are given a reading passage with a number of words missing from the sentences. The students must read the passage and fill in the blanks with the appropriate words to complete the sentences. I feel that this assessment is **invalid** because a child's reading ability involves a lot more than just [his or her] ability to fill in the blanks correctly. In no way does this test measure a child's ability to decode text, retell the story or answer questions about it, or self-monitor for breakdowns of comprehension. I feel that this assessment is **unreliable** because giving different versions of the test can result in very different scores. For example, if I give a child a passage about dinosaurs that is on a 4.0 reading level, and the child loves dinosaurs, then she will have a lot more background knowledge to pull from when it comes to understanding and completing the story, and will score higher on the test because of it. On the other hand, if I give that same child a passage about Ancient Rome that is on a 4.0 reading level, and the child knows nothing about the subject, then she will surely score lower than she would have on the dinosaur passage.

Katie
Elementary Teacher

TEACHER-TO-TEACHER
Validity and Reliability With One of My Students

As a special education teacher, I believe I have inadvertently given an assessment that is **unreliable**. This assessment was **unreliable** due to the nature of the test and the situation surrounding the test. This test was to measure a student's ability to read and complete mathematical computations. The student had been given the use of a calculator all year, and, on this particular day, she was asked to complete similar math problems *without* her calculator. The timing was also not conducive to getting quality results. The test was administered the day before Spring Break, with approximately 30 minutes left until the end of the school day. I believe this **skewed the results,** making the test an **unreliable judgment** of this student's ability and thereby leading to **inaccurate inferences** about her learning.

Nate
High School
Special Education Teacher

TEACHER-TO-TEACHER
Validity With One of My Students

Recently, a fourth-grade student was given a multiple choice history test and received a failing grade. This particular student reads on a third-grade level. While analyzing his test, I realized the test questions were written on an end-of-fourth-grade reading level and that he probably experienced great frustration just trying to read the questions. I re-administered the test orally, and the student was able to answer many of the questions correctly. I felt the initial administration of the test rendered the results **invalid** for this student because the test actually measured his ability to read the test questions and not his knowledge of history, which was the **intended outcome** of the instructional unit.

Ann
Elementary Teacher

TEACHER-TO-TEACHER
Validity and Reliability With My Students

A situation from my own experience in which I gave an assessment that was **invalid** was on a recent weekly spelling test. The purpose of the weekly spelling test was to assess the student's spelling of key terms. Students who memorized the list were able to score very high on the assessment, yet these same students would misspell the same or similar words in their writing assignments the very next week. Not only would the words be misspelled, the students were not able to recognize the misspelled words when proofreading their papers. The weekly spelling tests were more of an assessment of memorization skills than an indication of what I have come to realize was my **true intended learning outcome** for the students: not simply to spell the words correctly, but to do so in authentic writing situations.

Karen
Middle School
Technology Support Teacher

TEACHER-TO-TEACHER
Validity and Reliability With My Students

A personal experience as a teacher in which I gave an assessment that was **invalid** and **unreliable** was in summer school when I gave a group of rising 1st graders a pretest that was part of a series we were instructed to use. The series of questions was supposed to test shape acquisition of the square, heart, triangle, and circle. However, the set of questions was written in a table format that the children had never been exposed to. Needless to say, the majority of children got the shape questions wrong. However, when presented another way, all the children could identify those shapes. Another item in this math summer series was a parent guide that went right along with this preassessment. It let the parent know what their child needed to work on. In fact it was very specific. If the child missed the shape questions, I had to check a box that said your child could not identify those shapes. So, parents of these children naturally **inferred** that their children could not identify a heart, triangle, square or circle, when actually it was the table format that gave the child difficulty. Kids who knew their shapes just fine were not able to demonstrate their knowledge due to the format of the questions.

Lindsey
Elementary Teacher

TEACHER-TO-TEACHER
Validity and Reliability With My Students

As a teacher, there have been times in my own assessing of kids' work that I wish I had had greater **validity** and **reliability**. For example, I have often used poster projects as assessments of student learning in social studies, but haven't always clearly defined what a student's individual poster should contain in order to achieve a specific grade. Thus, an artistically pleasing poster that actually expressed very little mastery of content might receive a higher grade than would a blander-looking but more content-rich poster. There is a place for both types of posters in learning and expression, but where I fell short was in not specifying up front what the intention of the poster activity was. Neither my students nor I had any real clarity about *what* was most important for the posters to communicate about their learning. The lack of an assessment anchor such as a rubric also harmed **reliability**. I'm certain that I must have graded one group of posters differently from another because, for one group, I may have been rushed to finish or because I had a more negative or positive view of that class as a whole. Looking back, this is truly regretful, since the kids usually worked hard on their posters and definitely deserved a more professional effort in assessment.

Charley
Middle School
Social Studies Teacher

These teachers' reflections on their past practices and experiences with assessments in the classroom illustrate the core principles that should govern how we create and use tests in our classrooms. Teacher-made assessments must accurately represent what we believe them to represent about student learning, and assessments must do so in ways that dependably allow students with mastery of intended learning objectives to demonstrate that mastery through knowledge and skill rather than through chance. These core principles that govern the creation of classroom tests are *validity* and *reliability*, and they constitute meaningful assessments of student learning.

1   Joint Committee on Standards for Educational Evaluation. (2003). *The student evaluation standards.* Thousand Oaks, CA: Corwin.
2   Joint Committee on Standards for Educational Evaluation. (2003).
3   Joint Committee on Standards for Educational Evaluation. (2003).
4   Joint Committee on Standards for Educational Evaluation. (2003).
5   Angoff, W. H. (1988). Validity: An evolving concept. In H. Wainer, & H. I. Braun (Eds.) *Test validity.* Hillsdale, NJ: Lawrence Erlbaum Associates.
6   Stiggins, R. J., & Conklin, N. F. (1992). *In teachers' hands: Investigating the practices of classroom assessment.* Albany: State University of New York Press.
7   Angoff (1988).
8   Angoff (1988), p. 23.
9   Angoff (1988), p. 24.
10 Wainer, H., & Braun, H. I. (Eds.). (1988). *Test validity.* Hillsdale, NJ: Lawrence Erlbaum Associates.
11 Stiggins & Conklin (1992).
12 Marso, R. N., & Pigge, F. L. (1991). An analysis of teacher-made tests: Item types, cognitive demands, and item construction errors. *Contemporary Educational Psychology, 16,* 279–286.
13 Stiggins, R. (2006, November/December). Assessment for learning: A key to motivation and achievement. *Edge, 2*(2), 14.

3

How Do I
Create a Good Test?

Designing a good test is like building a house. You have to begin with the end in mind. You have to think about how it will look holistically and then think about how each part will look and how each part will function. To first build the house, you have to know what you want from the house. The same is true with a test. How should the test function? What information will be gleaned from the test? As with a house, creating a test involves first planning for the test itself.

This chapter focuses on building a test by first examining how content to be assessed can be determined and then by offering a systematic way of ensuring that curriculum, instruction, and assessment are aligned. Indeed, if these three components of teaching and learning are not aligned, then the information received from the test is flawed.

Figure 3.1 shows how the three elements of curriculum, instruction, and assessment form the sides of a triangle. In the figure, *curriculum* represents the intended curriculum—that is, what states and districts intend students to learn as is often expressed in a formal, written document. *Instruction* stands for the taught curriculum, that is, what the teacher actually teaches to the students. Finally, *assessment* focuses on the curriculum that is measured. Each element is at an apex of the triangle with arrows moving back and forth, indicating the need for alignment. Without each side, a triangle loses its structural integrity and cannot support itself. The same is true in teaching and learning. If the intended curriculum is not aligned with the taught curriculum, students may be missing critical knowledge and skills that they need to acquire. If the intended curriculum is not aligned with the assessments of learning, teachers cannot have a clear picture of students' knowledge and skills in terms of the expectations held in the written curriculum. If instruction is not aligned with assessment, students have not had the opportunity to learn the material for which they are held accountable and, therefore, the assessment is inherently unfair.

Figure 3.1. Curriculum Alignment

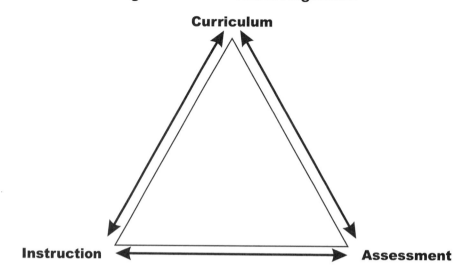

Any test must be aligned with both the content taught by teachers as well as the content teachers *intended* to teach. To this end, there are 10 essential steps involved in creating a test that is both valid and reliable (Figure 3.2).

Figure 3.2. Ten Steps in Designing a Good Test

☑ Step 1: Unpack the standards
☑ Step 2: Create a table of specifications
☑ Step 3: Clarify why, when, and where to assess students' learning
☑ Step 4: Determine types of assessment items to use
☑ Step 5: Determine number of assessment items to use
☑ Step 6: Write test items that are valid and reliable
☑ Step 7: Assemble the test
☑ Step 8: Construct a scoring key and/or rubric
☑ Step 9: Administer the test
☑ Step 10: Score the test and analyze the results

Steps 1 and 2 focus on the content of the test. Teachers must first unpack the state standards and instructional objectives for both the *content* and the *level of cognitive demand*. Then, teachers are ready to build a table of specifications using the information gleaned from unpacking standards and/or objectives. Step 3 addresses the conditions surrounding the testing situation. Questions such as, *Why am I administering this test? When will the test be administered?* and *Where will the test take place?* are considerations that affect the creation of a test. Steps 4 through 6 describe the importance of choosing the appropriate type and number of items to use and the critical step of writing test items that are both valid and reliable. A test is only as valid and reliable as the items contained within it. Step 7 involves assembling the test so that it is developmentally appropriate, user-friendly and free from grammatical and layout errors that can impact the reliability of the test. In Step 8, the scoring key and/or rubric is constructed so that teachers have a clear idea of the performance they expect on each item. Step 9 is the actual administration of the test. Teachers must ask themselves critical questions prior to the administration of the test, such as *Did I actually teach the information?* In the final step, the test is scored and the results are analyzed. This step provides valuable information regarding both the validity and reliability of the test. *Did most students provide an incorrect answer on one of the items? If so, what do teachers do about the item and the test score?* The steps in designing a good test involve not only the creation of the test, but the administration and analysis of test data as well. A test is only good if it yields useful information regarding student learning.

Step 1: Unpack the Standards

The first step in creating a valid and reliable assessment is to unpack the standards that are part of the intended or the written curriculum. **Unpacking the standards** is a phrase that describes the process of reviewing curricular objectives to identify the intended content and cognitive levels of learning for students. Unpacking the curriculum standards is the essential first step in ensuring alignment among curriculum, instruction, and assessment.

Curriculum, in today's environment, includes standards set by individual states. All 50 states have content standards in English, science, and mathematics; and 48 states have content standards in history.[1] Most school districts develop curriculum materials based on the established state standards so that students have an opportunity to perform well on the state assessment. They further delineate the state standards by breaking them down into discrete sets of information. This is part of a system in which state standards are translated into school district curricula. Teachers then, in turn, use the school district curriculum to address the standards in the classroom. This is part of both a horizontal and a vertical alignment of the curriculum.[2]

But, such *content standards* or *objectives* are oftentimes misinterpreted as consisting only of subject matter. A closer examination of content standards indicates that curricula actually include two main components: **content** and **level of cognitive demand.** Let's look at these two components of curriculum.

Content

Content is most often thought of as the subject matter to be delivered. Content can be explored in terms of three layers: explicit content, implicit content, and conditional content. The subject matter referred to in a standard is the **explicit content,** because it is evident simply by reading the standard itself. However, no content exists in isolation; all knowledge is connected with other knowledge. People learn, in part, by assimilating new knowledge into their existing understandings. In other words, students usually need prior knowledge of a topic as a prerequisite to learning more about that topic or before understanding it at a deeper level. When unpacking a curriculum standard, therefore, teachers also must be aware of this **implied content** knowledge—that is, knowledge students are presumed to have to engage in the explicit content of the standard. Finally, the content of many standards is also often dependent on certain circumstances or conditions, such as primary sources to be read or certain materials to be used. This type of content facilitates students' engagement with the explicit content of the standard and can be thought of as **conditional content.** In summary, most standards, or learning objectives, typically contain three content layers:

1. **Explicit content**: the subject matter directly referred to in the standard

2. **Implied content**: prior knowledge and skills students need to engage in the explicit content

3. **Conditional content**: specific circumstances, contexts, or conditions through which the student will engage with the explicit content

Each content layer must be addressed when planning for both instruction and assessment. To reiterate our earlier point, sometimes standards are taken at their face value—considering only explicit content—without taking into account both the implied and conditional content that facilitate learning. But taken together, the three content layers provide a more thorough interpretation of the standard and, therefore, of intended learning for students. Let's review an example by looking at the standard in Figure 3.3.

Figure 3.3. Content Contained Within Florida Sunshine State Mathematics Standard for Grades 3 to 5[3]

> The student uses and justifies <u>different estimation strategies in a real-world problem situation and determines the reasonableness of results of calculations in a given problem situation</u>.
>
> ### Analysis of Content Layers Within the Standard:
>
> - *Explicit Content*: different estimation strategies, reasonableness of calculations
> - *Implied Content*: rounding, adding, subtracting, multiplying, dividing
> - *Conditional Content*: in a real-world problem situation, in a given problem situation

To determine the content layers, we must first parse the content from the standard. We do this by asking ourselves, *What is the "what" of the standard? What are students expected to know and be able to do? What prior knowledge or skills should they have to engage with the "what"?* And, finally, *Under what conditions do they engage with the "what"?* Then, the content that we have identified in the standard is <u>underlined</u>.

Returning to our example, there are three questions we ask to identify the layers of content in the standard:

1. What is the explicit content?

   The explicit content contained in this standard includes both <u>estimation strategies</u> and <u>reasonableness of results of calculations</u>. This content is explicitly stated in the standard. It is the "what."

2. What is the implied content?

   To employ estimation strategies, students need to be able to <u>round numbers</u> and <u>carry out mathematical operations such as addition, subtraction, multiplication, and division</u>. These are the prerequisite skills that students need to have to estimate and evaluate the reasonableness of the calculations.

3. What is the conditional content?

   In this standard, students must use <u>given problem situations that reflect the real world</u> to demonstrate their ability to employ estimation strategies. This is a condition placed on how the students demonstrate their knowledge and skills; thus, it is conditional content.

To construct a valid and reliable test, teachers *must* have a deep understanding of the content. Understanding the nuances of the explicit, implicit, and conditional content is an important start but is not itself sufficient. Teachers must also be clear about the level of cognitive demand.

Level of Cognitive Demand

Unquestionably, human behavior and learning are inordinately complex, so any attempt to simplify our understanding of them ultimately falls short in some regard. Nevertheless, it is helpful to think of learning as a behavior and to think about the different domains in which people's behavior can be categorized. A broadly accepted understanding of behavior characterizes learning as taking place in three distinct domains: the cognitive domain, the psychomotor domain, and the affective domain.

Each domain of behavior is critical in its own right. The *cognitive domain* involves thinking and the acquisition of intellectual knowledge and skills. The *psychomotor domain* focuses on perceptual abilities and kinesthetics. In the *affective domain*, the focus is on values and judgments based on those values.

In formal education, the cognitive domain is the primary focus. Most teachers are familiar with Bloom's Taxonomy, which is a tool for classifying various levels of cognitive behavior. (There are also taxonomies for the psychomotor and affective domains.) Bloom's Taxonomy of Cognitive Behaviors consists of knowledge, comprehension, application, analysis, synthesis, and evaluation.[4] Figure 3.4 provides a description of the cognitive behaviors along with samples of appropriate verbs used when describing those behaviors. In recent years, others have offered revisions of Bloom's taxonomy.[5] While Bloom's remains most widely used, we offer in Figure 3.5 several cautions when using the cognitive taxonomy.[6]

Figure 3.4. Bloom's Taxonomy of Cognitive Behaviors[7]

Cognitive Level	Description This level of Bloom's Taxonomy focuses on…	Samples of Appropriate Behavioral Verbs			
Knowledge	Remembering facts, terms, or other specific knowledge	Count Define Describe Draw	Find Identify Label List	Locate Name State Recall	Recite Record Tell
Comprehension	Understanding meaning of content	Demonstrate Describe Discuss Explain	Give examples Identify Illustrate Interpret	Outline Paraphrase Predict Report	Restate Summarize Tell
Application	The ability to apply abstract meaning to novel, concrete situations	Apply Classify Compute	Determine Dramatize Draw Illustrate	Implement Prepare Select Show	Solve Transfer Use
Analysis	The ability to break down a whole into parts and understand the role of each part and the relationships among the parts	Analyze Break down Categorize Characterize	Compare Contrast Deduce Differentiate	Discriminate Distinguish Examine Infer	Investigate Relate Separate
Synthesis	Creating a new form with individual parts	Adapt Create Design Develop	Formulate Integrate Invent Imagine	Make Modify Perform Plan	Predict Produce Propose
Evaluation	Making judgments	Argue Assess Choose Conclude	Critique Decide Evaluate Judge	Justify Predict Prioritize Prove	Rank Rate Select

Figure 3.5. Cautions When Using a Taxonomy Such as Bloom's

Benjamin Bloom provided educators with a way to think about how students are taught information and the cognitive processes involved. However, there are some cautions when using Bloom's taxonomy, or any other taxonomy for that matter.

Not all standards fit neatly into one category. For example, the Florida Sunshine State Mathematics standard in Figure 3.3 overlaps into at least two cognitive levels: application and evaluation. One could also argue that to evaluate estimation strategies students must also be able to analyze the strategies and their uses; and, to analyze, students must have knowledge and comprehension of estimation strategies.

Taxonomies should not be viewed as strictly hierarchical in nature. By viewing *evaluation* at the top of the taxonomical heap, educators may mistakenly think that evaluation is better than application, and that application is better than knowledge. Again, the context (including student age, individual needs, and societal aims of the curriculum) determines the appropriate cognitive level.

Bloom is not the only one who has developed a taxonomy of cognitive behaviors. A recently revised version of Bloom's taxonomy expands the understanding of "knowledge" and uses somewhat different terms to describe cognitive behaviors.[8] Teachers may decide that a different taxonomy is more appropriate to use in their setting or for their content. For example, the following taxonomical levels were developed specifically for mathematics[9]:

- Memorize
- Perform procedures
- Demonstrate understanding
- Conjecture, generalize, prove
- Solve nonroutine problems, make connections

Regardless, teachers should use some grounded version of a cognitive taxonomy to provide a framework for determining the level of cognitive demand in their respective curricula.

Most verbs have different meanings in different contexts. For example, the verb *identify* is listed under both the *knowledge* and *comprehension* levels of cognitive demand in Figure 3.4. The cognitive level is determined by knowing the context within which students will identify. The Nevada State Standard for Grade 5 Health in Figure 3.8 provides a case in point. In this standard, students are to "identify" stated and implied messages within an advertisement. This type of behavior actually suggests *analysis* because students must interpret the explicit and implicit content of the advertisements for both types of messages.

Bloom's taxonomy addresses the cognitive domain only and not the affective and psychomotor domains. The focus of this book is on the cognitive domain of learning. This is not to say that the other two domains—affective and psychomotor domains—are any less important. For example, we not only want our students to be able to read, we want to them to enjoy reading. We want our students to be able to classify types of art as well as develop an appreciation for art. Appreciation and enjoyment are inherently affective in nature. The affective domain reaches aims of education that are often intangible—lifelong learning and productive citizenship, for example. These are values or beliefs that get at the heart of schooling, which is to prepare students for life in broader society. However, such intended outcomes of schooling are oftentimes difficult, if not impossible, to measure. The psychomotor domain is no less important. To be able to write, a student must be able to hold a pencil in his hand. Although the affective and psychomotor domains are a part of the content that students learn in school, they are usually not tested using paper-pencil format and so are not addressed directly in this book.

The first column of Figure 3.4 lists the cognitive levels of Bloom's taxonomy. The second column provides a description of the cognitive level, and the third column provides examples of verbs that may be used in state standards or instructional objectives. These verbs suggest the cognitive behaviors associated with a given standard or objective. The level of cognitive demand addresses the question, *What is the observable behavior associated with the expected cognitive activity?* For example, is the student expected to identify continents on a world map? Evaluate President Truman's decision to drop the atomic bomb? Analyze a short story for symbolism?

Essentially, the **level of cognitive demand** is the expected level of thinking when engaged with the content. The inclusion of the level of cognitive demand is critical when unpacking standards. Indeed, when researchers in one study set out to examine the effects of content coverage on student achievement, they were able to account for more of the changes in student achievement when they included both the content *and* the level of cognitive demand.[10] The level of cognitive demand completes the overall content picture. Instead of merely focusing on the subject matter being taught, the focus also includes what students do with the subject matter. For example, in English class students may be required to memorize and recite various forms of poetry. This is at the recall, or knowledge, level. However, if students are to interpret the figurative language of a poem, the students must interact with the subject matter at a higher cognitive level—at least at the analysis level in this example. When creating tests, both the subject matter and the cognitive level of the questions should reflect the intended learning outcomes articulated within the curriculum.

Let's apply this concept of level of cognitive demand to the Florida Sunshine State Mathematics example repeated in Figure 3.6. The levels of cognitive demand in the standard are circled as shown below. Three verbs in the standard provide a clue as to the cognitive behaviors that are being asked of students: uses, justifies, and determines. *Use* implies that students apply estimation strategies and thus this part of the standard requires application-level cognitive behavior. *Justify* implies evaluation, because students must be able to defend the use of various estimation strategies. *Determine* also suggests evaluation because students must critique an answer to know if it is reasonable. This standard is targeting higher cognitive levels for upper elementary students.

Figure 3.6. Levels of Cognitive Demand of Florida Sunshine State Mathematics Standard for Grades 3 to 5[11]

The student uses and justifies different estimation strategies in a real-world problem situation and determines the reasonableness of results of calculations in a given problem situation.

When identifying the cognitive level of a learning objective, it is important neither to overestimate nor underestimate the level of cognitive demand required within a standard. For example, consider the state standard in Figure 3.7.

Figure 3.7. Virginia State Standard of Learning, Grade 8 English[12]

> The student writes in a variety of forms including narrative, expository, persuasive, and informational.

When examining this standard, we immediately know the content, which is narrative, expository, persuasive, and informational essays. And the action verb in this standard is evident enough, too: write. This verb, by itself, implies that the standard is written at the application level, because students are most likely taught how to write these types of essays and then they apply this knowledge to writing their own essays. However, this underestimates the standard. Think about the persuasive essay, for example. This type of essay requires students to weigh competing evidence, consider an audience's perspective, and develop a reasoned argument. Clearly, this standard is tapping the upper levels of Bloom's taxonomy beyond the level of application. Underestimating or overestimating the level of cognitive demand can distort the way a teacher teaches the content and, ultimately, can affect the nature and degree of student learning with regard to any given learning objective or standard.

Putting It Together

In the previous two sections, we examined the content and level of cognitive demand independently. Now we will examine them together using examples from state standards. Figure 3.8 demonstrates how state standards from various disciplines are unpacked in terms of content and level of cognitive demand. Notice how the content layers—explicit, implicit, and conditional—are first determined. Then, the level of cognitive demand for each standard is identified using the verbs in the standards. Next, those verbs are correlated with the cognitive levels in Bloom's Taxonomy.

Figure 3.8. Sample Standards Unpacked

Standard	Content[14,15,16,17]	Verbs Used to Indicate Level of Cognitive Demand	Bloom's Classification
California State Standard, Grade 7 Music [13] Analyze the use of form in a varied repertoire of music representing diverse genres, styles, and cultures	**Explicit Content** Use of form in a varied repertoire of music including diverse genres, styles, and cultures **Implied Content** Knowledge of the diverse genres, styles, and cultures **Conditional Content** Varied repertoire of music	Analyze	Analysis
Wisconsin State Standard, Grade 12 Economics [14] Use basic economic concepts (such as supply and demand; production, distribution, and consumption; labor, wages, and capital; inflation and deflation; market economy and command economy) to compare and contrast local, regional, and national economies across time and at the present time	**Explicit Content** Basic economic concepts (e.g., supply and demand; production, distribution, and consumption; labor, wages, and capital; inflation and deflation; market economy and command economy); local, regional, and national economies across time and the present time **Implied Content** Knowledge of types of economies **Conditional Content** Use basic economic concepts	Use Compare Contrast	Application Analysis
Nevada State Standards, Grade 5 Health [15] Analyze the influence of culture, media, technology, and other factors on health by examining an advertisement for a food or health-related product and identify stated and implied messages	**Explicit Content** Influence of culture, media, technology, and other factors on health; stated and implied messages **Implied Content** Knowledge of advertisements and their purposes; an understanding of culture, media, and technology **Conditional Content** Advertisement for a food or health product	Analyze Examine Identify	Analysis
Maryland Voluntary State Curriculum, Grade 7 Writing [16] Describe in prose and/or poetic forms to clarify, extend, or elaborate on ideas by using evocative language and appropriate organizational structure to create a dominant expression	**Explicit Content** Prose and poetic forms to create a dominant expression **Implied Content** How to write in prose or poetry Evocative language Appropriate organizational structure **Conditional Content** Use evocative language and appropriate organizational structure	Describe Use Create	Knowledge Comprehension Application Analysis Evaluation Synthesis

Step 2: Create a Table of Specifications

In the beginning of the chapter, designing a good test was likened to building a house. A table of specifications described here is much like a blueprint of a house in that the blueprint provides the design of the house to be built. In fact, a table of specifications is often referred to in the assessment field as a "test blueprint."[17] A **table of specifications** is a chart or table that details the content and level of cognitive demand assessed on a test as well as the types and emphases of test items.

A table of specifications is essential to addressing both validity and reliability. Validity, as explained earlier, means that the assessment can be used to draw appropriate inferences. A table of specifications provides a way to ensure that the assessment is based on the intended outcomes of learning as articulated in the curriculum and on instruction that students received. Reliability means that we can have confidence in the results of the assessment because the assessment guards against systematic error. A table of specifications also provides a way of ensuring that the number of questions on a test is adequate to ensure dependable results that are not likely caused by chance. Here we look at creating a table of specifications to guide the building of a test.

Unpacking the Standards

Creating a table of specifications involves first unpacking the standards to determine what students should know and be able to do, which we described previously in Step 1. The next step is then to map out the intersection between the content and the level of cognitive demand. Let's review an example. Phyllis Phylum teaches fifth grade. She will be teaching a 4-week unit on the classification of organisms. Her school district developed objectives based on state standards for fifth-grade science. Phyllis uses the district's pacing guide to map out the 4-week unit to determine the number of instructional days that will be spent on specific content. Figure 3.9 shows the objectives along with the number of instructional days spent on each set of objectives and the percentage of instructional time within the 4-week period.[18]

Figure 3.9. Educational Objectives From a Four-Week Unit (20 Instructional Days) in the Life Sciences (Fifth Grade)

The student will:

1. Compare and contrast key features and activities between organisms (10 days/50%).
   a. Classify organisms based on physical features.
   b. Arrange organisms in a hierarchy according to similarities and differences in features.
   c. Categorize examples of organisms as representatives of the kingdoms and recognize that the number of kingdoms is subject to change.
2. Recognize scientific names as part of a binomial nomenclature (2 days/10%).
3. Recognize examples of major animal phyla (4 days/20%).
4. Recognize examples of major plant phyla. (4 days/20%)

Now let's unpack the standards of Phyllis' unit. The content of these standards include the following:

- ◆ Key features and activities between organisms
  - • Physical features of organisms
  - • Hierarchical system of organism
  - • Organisms as representatives of the kingdoms
- ◆ Scientific names as part of a binomial nomenclature
- ◆ Major animal phyla
- ◆ Major plant phyla

The verbs in the standards give us information on the level of cognitive demand required throughout the unit. The verbs include the following:

- ◆ Compare
- ◆ Contrast
- ◆ Classify
- ◆ Categorize
- ◆ Recognize

Using Bloom's taxonomy of cognitive behaviors (see Figure 3.4 again) as our interpretive framework, we can see that the verbs within the standard suggest that students are intended to analyze, apply, comprehend, and recall content knowledge about organisms.

Mapping Objectives

Now that the standards have been unpacked, the next task is to map out the objectives on a table. In Figure 3.10, the content is located in the left-hand column and the cognitive levels are located across the top row. The key is to find the intersection between both content and the level of cognitive demand and then to indicate the intersection between the two. For example, in the first objective, the content is "key features and activities between organisms." The level of cognitive demand is indicated by the verbs *compare* and *contrast*. These two verbs tell Phyllis that *analysis* is required. Therefore, a ✓ has been placed on the grid where *analysis* and *key features of organisms* intersect in Figure 3.10. However, to analyze key features of organisms, students must have knowledge of the key features and understand the meanings of the key features, indicating *knowledge* and *comprehension*. They must then *apply* the key features to organisms to compare and contrast them. Hence, Phyllis placed a √ in the knowledge, comprehension, application, and analysis levels as well. Phyllis repeated the process for the other objectives. It is important to note here that not all of the possible intersections of content and cognitive level are checked. Notice in Figure 3.10 that students are *not* intended to master the content at the *synthesis* or *evaluation* levels, nor should they be according to the objectives. Therefore, the assessment for this unit should not contain any items that require synthesis or evaluation.

Figure 3.10. Table of Specifications for 4-Week Unit Test on Life Sciences (Grade 5)

Content	Level of Cognitive Demand					
	Knowledge	Comprehension	Application	Analysis	Synthesis	Evaluation
Organisms (50%) • Key Features • Physical Features • Kingdoms	✓	✓	✓	✓		
Scientific Names (10%)	✓	✓				
Animal Phyla (20%)	✓	✓	✓	✓		
Plant Phyla (20%)	✓	✓	✓	✓		

Determining Emphasis

The next step in developing a table of specifications for a test is to determine the relative *emphasis* of content at each level of cognitive demand. This emphasis may come from an examination of the emphasis given to a specific content on a state assessment, as well as the emphasis the content was given in class. One way to gauge emphasis is to determine how many instructional days were spent on particular content and at a particular level of cognitive demand. Also, emphasis can be determined by the significance or the importance of the content or skill within the subject area. It is at this point that expertise in the subject matter is critical. For example, in Figure 3.10 we can see that identifying key features, physical features, and kingdoms has been given greater emphasis in instruction—50%, or about half, of the total instructional time. It follows then that the test developed by Phyllis should reflect that percentage. Using a simple nominal scale of low, moderate, and high emphasis, Phyllis can indicate the relative degree of emphasis on certain objectives.

Phyllis then has to examine the percentage of instruction that focused on the level of cognitive demand. Now Phyllis can go back and determine relative emphasis by indicating whether the content was given low, moderate, or high emphasis. Figure 3.11 shows the emphasis Phyllis gave to the content within the 4-week unit. Based on lesson plans, pacing guides, and the number of days actually spent on the content, Phyllis determined that the emphasis on organisms as a general category was high throughout the unit because it provided the basis for the rest of the content. It is also clear that little instruction in animal and plant phyla occurred at the application and analysis levels but focused more on the knowledge and comprehension levels.

Figure 3.11. Blueprint for 4-Week Unit Test on Life Sciences With Emphasis (Grade 5)

Content	Level of Cognitive Demand					
	Knowledge	Comprehension	Application	Analysis	Synthesis	Evaluation
Organisms (50%) • Key Features • Physical Features • Kingdoms	H	H	H	H		
Scientific Names (10%)	M	M				
Animal Phyla (20%)	M	M	L	L		
Plant Phyla (20%)	M	M	L	L		

Scale of Instructional Emphasis: L = Low Emphasis M = Moderate Emphasis H = High Emphasis

Although a teacher could sit and examine numbers and percentages to determine whether emphasis on content was low, moderate, or high, the reality is that as a content expert Phyllis can estimate emphasis by knowing which content received more instructional time or is deemed more important than other content. Whatever the approach used to develop emphasis in the table of specifications, the number and types of questions that ultimately appear on the assessment depend in large part on a teacher's determination of emphasis.

Step 3: Clarify Why, When, and Where to Assess Students' Learning

Steps 1 and 2 focused on *what* to assess. Just as important, however, is to focus on *why*, *when*, *where*, and *under what conditions* to assess. In building a house, such questions are critical. Will the house be a starter home for a new family or will the house be a retirement home? Where will the house be built? These questions provide information that is critical when planning for a house. These aspects of testing provide the context within which the assessment will take place. The context provides information regarding the uses of the assessment data and provides parameters in developing the assessment. When developing any assessment, you should ask the following questions:

◆ Why and when am I assessing students?

As discussed in Chapter 1, assessment is used for three purposes. These include preassessment, formative assessment, and summative assessment. Teachers may desire to find out where students may have strengths and deficiencies. In this case, teachers determine where students are prior to instruction. Formative assessments typically occur during instruction. Teachers use formative assessments to determine whether students are learning the incremental skills necessary to accomplish a task and then use the assessment data to adjust instruction. Summative assessments occur at the end of instruction. Teachers do need summary information to give an indication of whether students have accomplished a specific skill or learned certain material.

The *when* of assessing students is inextricably related to the *why*. The purpose of the assessment will determine when the assessment should take place. For example, if an assessment is to be used for formative purposes and yet is administered and shared with students after the summative assessment, the formative information is not useful to either students or teachers.

- ◆ Where and under what conditions will I assess students?

Conditions of testing can include the venue for the assessment, the time period in which the assessment takes place, and the help that teachers give to students during the test. The venue is driven by the purposes and type of the assessment. For example, an English teacher may wish to assess oral speaking skills. The most appropriate and authentic way to assess these skills is by having students actually give a speech in front of an audience and to assess the students' ability based on a rubric. This is more authentic than having a student watch a speech and critique it. The venue in this case is in the classroom or some other place in which the presentations will take place. The venue could be a basketball court if students are to demonstrate basketball skills. Typically, for paper-pencil tests the venue is the classroom.

Teachers also need to determine how much time students have to complete the assessment. The amount of time is influenced by the type of assessment. Some project-based assessments may take a week, two weeks, or even an entire semester. A paper-and-pencil test might be administered in one class period, and a multiple choice test may be the best option because of time constraints. The determination of time can also be influenced by how long teachers have to spend on a particular unit of study. Many school districts use pacing guides or curriculum maps that teachers must follow.

Teachers must also determine how much help will be given and then must be consistent in providing only the amount of predetermined assistance. This is important because sometimes teachers may provide information to students that they actually want to assess whether the students know. This can be a common error because teachers oftentimes want to support their students' thinking and provide their students every possibility to succeed. Although these are good intentions, to be sure, teachers must be careful not to introduce systematic error into a testing situation by providing a student so much assistance that the results are no longer an accurate reflection of the student's learning. It's worth noting that this same principle applies to accommodating the needs of students with learning disabilities. Although there are entire resources devoted to this topic, we simply caution here that accommodations, like teacher assistance, should be appropriate to the inferences that an assessment is intended to provide evidence of.

Returning to our example, Phyllis Phylum has made these choices in developing her test. She will use the test for summative purposes to determine whether students have learned the material. The students receive grades on the test and those grades are used as one data source to determine the students' 9-weeks grades in science. Phyllis has also determined that she will use a paper-pencil test with objective type questions because of time constraints, the need for efficiency, and the nature of the content. Ahead of time she decides to provide help only by clarifying questions on the test. She determines that if one student needs clarification on a question, she will share the same clarification with all of the students. Phyllis has considered *why, when, where,* and *under what conditions* this particular test will occur; and her decisions contribute to the design of the test and, therefore, to the inferences about student learning she will be able to draw from the results.

Step 4: Determine Types of Assessment Items

Next, teachers must decide what types of items to include on the test. There are two basic types of items: *select-response* and *supply-response*. With select-response items, the student chooses from answer choices provided by teachers. These items include true-false, matching, and multiple choice. Figure 3.12 shows these types of select-response items on a continuum of student response options. True-false questions provide students with only two response options, whereas matching and multiple choice have more than two response options. Matching is placed in the middle of the continuum, as a matching set typically results in options being narrowed as they are used.

Figure 3.12. Types of Select-Response Items

True-False	Matching	Multiple Choice

By way of contrast, supply-response items require that the student provide the answers to questions. Supply-response items include fill-in-the-blank, short answer, computation, essay, performance task, project, and original creation. Figure 3.13 shows the continuum of supply-response items. Student responses for the fill-in-the-blank and short answer are typically predetermined by the question being posed. In other words, the range of probable responses is typically restricted with these two types of items. However, as you move to the right of the continuum the response is more open-ended. (Notably, fill-in-the-blank questions for which a *word bank* is provided essentially function the same as matching questions, within the select-response family of question types.)

Figure 3.13. Types of Supply-Response Items

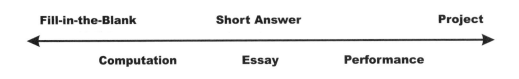

The type(s) of questions chosen to include on a test can depend on a myriad of factors including, but not limited to, the time allotted for the test, the content, and level of cognitive demand being assessed. Figure 3.14 indicates the amount of time each type of question may take to answer and the level of cognitive demand that can be assessed. Because testing is always a question of sampling a limited set of behaviors to represent broader behaviors, considering these practical issues of the typical time needed to respond to items is wise.

Phyllis decides to use multiple choice, fill-in-the-blank, short answer, and essay items on her test. Phyllis reasons that she can assess the multiple cognitive levels identified in her objectives using these types of questions. Also, she determines the test item types appropriate for the content being tested, while balancing her concern about the time students have to complete the test within the 55-minute science period. Therefore, she chooses the most efficient question types to include.

Figure 3.14. Question Types by Level of Cognitive Demand and Time Constraints[19]

Type of Question	How Long It Takes to Answer	Levels of Cognitive Demand that Can be Assessed: Knowledge	Comprehension	Application	Analysis	Synthesis	Evaluation
Selected Response							
• Multiple Choice	30 to 60 seconds*	✓	✓	✓	✓		
• True-False	15 seconds	✓	✓				
• Matching	60–90 seconds+	✓	✓				
Supply Response							
• Fill-in-the-Blank	30 seconds	✓	✓	✓	✓		
• Short Answer	30–45 seconds	✓	✓	✓	✓		✓
• Essay	At least 60 seconds for each individual point; significant additional time may be needed	✓	✓	✓	✓	✓	✓

✶ depending on the level of cognitive demand.
+ depending on number of matching items.

Step 5: Determine the Number of Assessment Items, by Type

Now that Phyllis has determined which types of questions to use, she returns to the table of specifications, indicating the types of test questions and number of test questions per intersection of content and level of cognitive demand. In Figure 3.15 Phyllis plots the type of question and the number of questions within the table of specifications. The number of items in each cell of the table of specifications provides us with evidence related to reliability. Notice that Phyllis has only one question for the content *animal phyla* at the *application* level. One concern with having only one question within this particular cell is that the possibility of systematic error can greatly skew the results. Phyllis is placing faith in *one* item to provide an indication of whether students know this content at this particular cognitive level. However, Phyllis now has a 41-question test, and she feels that she cannot include more questions because of the developmental level of her students. These are decisions that Phyllis must make, but she recognizes the consequences of her decisions.

Once Phyllis plots the number and type of test questions, she has a blueprint to follow. The division of test items throughout the table of specifications is based on relative emphasis, and she knows the types of questions to develop based on the intersection between content and level of cognitive demand. A template of a table of specifications is included at the end of the chapter for use in designing your own tests. However, do not let the formality fool you. A table of specifications can be sketched out on a napkin or a scrap piece of paper. Creating a table of specifications is a simple matter of showing the intersection between content and level of cognitive demand, and then ensuring that you have questions that assess those points of intersection. Just as important, however, is being sure that your test does not include items or content at a level of cognitive demand *not* indicated on your table of specifications.

Figure 3.15. Blueprint for 4-Week Unit Test on Life Sciences with Emphasis, Type, and Number of Questions (Grade 5)

Content (% of instructional time)	Level of Cognitive Demand					
	Knowledge	Comprehension	Application	Analysis	Synthesis	Evaluation
Organisms Key Features Physical Features Kingdoms (50%)	Emphasis: Strong # & Type of Test Items: 6 Fill-in-the-Blank	Emphasis: Strong # & Type of Test Items: 6 Multiple Choice	Emphasis: Strong # & Type of Test Items: 4 Multiple Choice 1 Short Answer	Emphasis: Strong # & Type of Test Items: 2 Multiple Choice 1 Essay		
Scientific Names (10%)	Emphasis: Moderate # & Type of Test Items: 3 Multiple Choice	Emphasis: Moderate # & Type of Test Items: 2 Short Answer				
Animal Phyla (20%)	Emphasis: Moderate # & Type of Test Items: 2 Multiple Choice 1 Short Answer	Emphasis: Moderate # & Type of Test Items: 1 Multiple Choice 1 Short Answer	Emphasis: Low # & Type of Test Items: 1 Multiple Choice	Emphasis: Low # & Type of Test Items: 1 Multiple Choice		
Plant Phyla (20%)	Emphasis: Moderate # & Type of Test Items: 4 Fill-in-the-Blank	Emphasis: Moderate # & Type of Test Items: 3 Multiple Choice	Emphasis: Low # & Type of Test Items: 1 Multiple Choice	Emphasis: Low # & Type of Test Items: 1 Multiple Choice		

Step 6: Write Test Items
That Are Valid and Reliable

A test is only as valid and reliable as the items within it. Test items should assess content and levels of cognitive demand contained on the table of specifications. Here are a few questions to ask as you write items:

- ◆ Does the item address the appropriate content, at the appropriate cognitive level?
- ◆ Does the item distinguish between those who have learned the standard or objective and those who have not?
- ◆ Are all items free from systematic error?

The first question relates to the *content validity* of the item. In other words, do your test items assess what you intend for them to assess? The second and third questions relate to the reliability of the item. Because it is important that individual test items be both valid and reliable, we devote Chapters 4 and 5 to a complete and practical discussion of writing test items. Suffice it to say here that you want your test questions to assess what you think they assess, and you want them to do so in a way that ensures that a student has every opportunity to demonstrate learning, with minimal influence of chance or error.

Step 7: Assemble the Test

This next step may seem unnecessary, but it is actually critical in ensuring the reliability of the test. The physical layout of your test and the attention to detail that is required can help ensure that students have the best opportunity to demonstrate their knowledge and that the layout of the test is not a source of confusion. A few central guidelines follow.

Make Sure That One Item Does Not Give Away the Answer to Another Item

Have you ever taken a test, struggled with a question, and found the answer to that question later in the test? As a student, you were probably delighted that now you had the answer; but, as a teacher, you know that now the reliability of the item is called into question. The student (you, in this case!) had the correct answer because of error in the test, not necessarily because of knowledge.

Provide Clear Directions for Each Portion of the Test

Clear directions let a student know what to do. For example, on a matching set the directions may state that a student may use an item more than once or that an item may be used only once. These directions are critical for the student to complete the test and could mean the difference between demonstrating learning or not.

Place Individual Test Items on One Full Page

An item or a set of items should be placed on the same page or on facing pages. If not, a student may not understand that more options are located on subsequent pages. For example, if two of the four answer choices in a multiple choice item are placed on a different page, a student may think that the only two options are those placed under the item stem. Therefore, the student may answer the question incorrectly because of the placement of the answer choices, not because of the student's knowledge of the subject matter.

Make Sure the Test Is Neat and Error Free

The test should be organized with clear breaks between sections and space between items to indicate to the student that a new item has begun. A grammatical error on a test may give a student a clue about the correct answer in a multiple choice item, or it may confuse the student into thinking that the correct response is incorrect because it does not grammatically complete the item stem. Ask a colleague to review the test to make sure the test is free from error.

Provide Clear and Adequate Response Spaces

Answer spaces that are clearly indicated are important so that students understand where they are to place their responses. For example, you may provide a line next to each multiple choice item for student responses. For supply-response items, students need adequate space to supply the response. The space needed is determined by the grade level and the length of response required to adequately answer the question.

Provide Point Values for Older Students

Older students can benefit from knowing how many points each item is worth. Providing points helps students self-assess their own performance on the test and can help students to strategize as they take a test.

Organize the Test by Item Type Format

Tests should be organized by item type format. For example, all multiple choice items should be together, all true-false items should be together, and so forth. The type of thinking required for each item type is different. Switching between multiple choice, true-false, and fill-in-the-blank, for example, requires students to readjust their thinking with each type of question. This is unnecessary and easily avoided by grouping questions by item type.

Assembling the test requires time and thought. The organization and look of the test should contribute to the reliability of the test and to student performance—and detract from neither.

Step 8: Construct a Scoring Key and/or Rubric

A scoring key created prior to the administration of the assessment provides the individual grading the assessment with parameters. Without the scoring key, two individuals grading the same test may come to different conclusions based on their own views of the importance of the information. The scoring key should indicate point values for each item and how a final score will be figured. Let's take, for example, the grade 5 science test being constructed in this chapter. In Phyllis' school, grades are determined through numbers. Performance on class work, homework, tests, and quizzes are translated into point values with a range of 0 to 100. These point values are averaged into a final 9-week average, which is then translated into a letter grade.

Figure 3.16 shows how Phyllis divides the point values for each type of test item. There are a total of 41 items on the test, with the multiple choice constituting the bulk of the items. Notice that multiple choice items and fill-in-the-blank are scored at 2 points each, whereas the short answer and essay are scored at 4 and 10 points, respectively. The points assigned to the various portions correspond with the emphasis and instructional time spent on the content. The content with the highest emphases have higher point values, and the content with the lower emphases have lower point values. Although the point values assigned do not represent exact percentages, the total points do reflect the approximate emphases of the content. This is an important point: The number of points assigned within the table of specifications should reflect the relative emphasis. That is, more points should be awarded for content with higher emphases.

Figure 3.16. Point Values Assigned to Each Test Item

Item Type	Number of Items	Points per Item	Total Points
Multiple Choice	25	2	50
Fill-in-the-Blank	10	2	20
Short Answer	5	4	20
Essay	1	10	10
TOTAL	41	–	100

A scoring rubric must also be constructed to score the essay portion of this test. The scoring rubric must define the essential criteria in the student response and the point values assigned for those essential criteria. In this case Phyllis has assigned a point value of 10 to the essay. She must now determine how these 10 points will be earned. A thorough discussion of rubric development is provided in Chapter 5, in which the focus is on developing supply-response items such as essay, short answer, and performance tasks that require rubrics for scoring. The rubric ensures both the validity and reliability of the test results.

Step 9: Administer the Test

The next step is to actually administer the test. When administering tests, teachers should standardize the conditions as much as possible. Typically, each student has the same amount of time, test, and type of assistance during the test administration. However, standardization does not trump a student's needs. As suggested previously in this chapter, an Individualized Educational Plan (IEP) for a student may indicate that the student requires more time to complete tests or may require that all tests be read to the student. Teachers must take into account these considerations in standardization.

Regardless of the purpose or type of test, there are a few questions that a teacher can ask and answer prior to administering an assessment. These questions are intended to ensure the alignment of curriculum, instruction, and assessment:

- Did I teach this information?
- Did I teach at the level of cognitive demand required in the test questions?

◆ What should I do if I did not teach some information?

Any teacher knows that plans do change, and sometimes the instruction that is planned is changed for a myriad of reasons including interruptions to the school schedule and student difficulty with the information. Many school districts use pacing guides and teachers are expected to spend only a certain amount of time on each unit of study; nevertheless, a teacher must account for possible changes in pacing.

In our life sciences example, Phyllis had 4 weeks to teach this information and then she had to move on to the next unit. At the end of the 4 weeks she may have realized that she did not cover some of the information. She essentially has two options. First, she can delete questions that address content not covered and reconfigure the test, or she can wait to administer the test until she has covered the content. The advantage of deleting questions is that Phyllis can stay on track with her school district's pacing guide. The disadvantage of deleting the questions is that she has then compromised the validity of the test. It no longer fits the table of specifications. Another disadvantage is that she may not have covered content required by the state, which can have consequences later when a student takes the state assessment. If Phyllis waits to administer the test, the table of specifications remains intact and validity is not compromised. She has also provided her students with the opportunity to learn for which they will be held accountable. However, if she waits to administer the test, she will be further behind according to her district's pacing guide and may not get to other important content later in the year, thus negatively affecting a student's opportunity to learn the information. These are decisions that teachers must make every time they plan for and assess learning, and the answers are not always clear. As a professional teacher, however, you should be fully aware of the trade-offs of whatever decision you deem most appropriate in a situation you may face.

Step 10: Score the Test and Analyze the Results

Steps 9 and 10 may seem odd to include in designing a good test, but the design and interpretation of any test demands that results be examined to determine whether the items were both valid and reliable. Although major test publishing companies use statistical analyses to make this determination, teachers can conduct a quick *item analysis* using the table of specifications created when designing the test. Teachers can identify frequently missed items as well as items with perfect or near-perfect responses. In conducting the item analysis, teachers ask themselves three essential questions:

1. What patterns regarding frequently missed responses emerge?
2. Is each item free from systematic error?
3. Were the content and cognitive level adequately addressed in class?

After these questions have been answered, teachers then decide whether to adjust scoring of the assessment, adjust instruction, and/or reteach. In this way, the assessment results can be used for further learning.

Look at an example of an item analysis from our fifth-grade science test. Phyllis has 25 students in her class. Figure 3.17 shows how students performed on each question as a class. For multiple choice and fill-in-the-blank items, the number of incorrect responses is indicated. For the short answer and essay questions, the average number of points earned is indicated.

Overall, Phyllis is pleased with the results. Most students earned 75% or better on the test, with a few not performing very well. In examining the number of incorrect responses, Phyllis notices a pattern. The students had the most difficulty with analysis and key features, physical features, and kingdoms of organisms. She notes that they performed well at the lower cognitive levels. Eight students (or 32%) missed question 24, and six students (or 24%) missed question 25. The average number of points earned on the essay was seven. Phyllis would have liked slightly higher scores on the essay. Now Phyllis must make the decision about to what to do with this information. She could go back and reteach at the analysis level, or she could move on to the next unit of study, making a note to address this issue next year.

Phyllis also looks at items that have perfect responses. All students responded to items 13 and 31 correctly. After examining these items, Phyllis determines that item 13 has some error in it, because the other answer choices are not plausible. So she realizes that item 13 is not a reliable test question. Phyllis could throw out the item and recalculate the students' grades, but she does not think it's a good idea to change a student's grade for the worse because it can have the consequence of discouraging students and seeming unfair to them. Phyllis recognizes, however, that she cannot draw inferences about student learning based on this one item. However, notice that she has six multiple choice items that assess the same content at the same level of cognitive demand. So, she has the other five items on which to base her inferences. In item 31, no error is detected and Phyllis determines that all students knew the correct answer.

Figure 3.17. Number of Incorrect Responses, by Item

Content	Level of Cognitive Demand					
	Knowledge	Comprehension	Application	Analysis	Synthesis	Evaluation
Organisms Key Features Physical Features Kingdoms (50%)	6 Fill-in-the-Blank Items Item 26: 2 incorrect Item 27: 3 incorrect Item 28: 4 incorrect Item 29: 2 incorrect Item 30: 1 incorrect Item 31: 0 incorrect	6 Multiple Choice Items Item 3: 5 incorrect Item 4: 2 incorrect Item 12: 1 incorrect Item 13: 0 incorrect Item 19: 2 incorrect Item 20: 3 incorrect	4 Multiple Choice Items Item 14: 2 incorrect Item 15: 1 incorrect Item 21: 6 incorrect Item 22: 4 incorrect 1 Short Answer Item Item 40: 3 points earned, on average	2 Multiple Choice Items Item 24: 8 incorrect Item 25: 6 incorrect 1 Essay Item 41: 7 points earned, on average		
Scientific Names (10%)	3 Multiple Choice Items Item 1: 3 incorrect Item 2: 5 incorrect Item 18: 16 incorrect	2 Short Answer Items Item 36: 2 incorrect Item 37: 3 incorrect				
Animal Phyla (20%)	2 Multiple Choice Items Item 10: 2 incorrect Item 11: 4 incorrect 1 Short Answer Item Item 39: 3.8 points earned, on average	1 Multiple Choice Item Item 9: 2 incorrect 1 Short Answer Item Item 38: 3.5 points earned, on average	1 Multiple Choice Item Item 5: 8 incorrect	1 Multiple Choice Item Item 6: 3 incorrect		
Plant Phyla (20%)	4: Fill-in-the-Blank Item 32: 2 incorrect Item 33: 3 incorrect Item 34: 4 incorrect Item 35: 3 incorrect	3: Multiple Choice Item 7: 3 incorrect Item 8: 5 incorrect Item 23: 4 incorrect	1: Multiple Choice Item 16: 2 incorrect	1: Multiple Choice Item 17: 2 incorrect		

One item has a high number of incorrect responses, and that is item 18. Sixteen (or 64%) of the students responded incorrectly to the item. After looking at the item, Phyllis determines that three of the answer choices could be correct. So now she must decide what to do with this information. Remember, Phyllis has a policy that grade changes can only help students and not hurt them. She decides to throw out the item and recalculate the students' grades. Because of the problem with item 18, she now has only two items on which to draw inferences for knowledge of scientific names.

Analyzing test results gives teachers a great deal of information regarding what students know and have learned as well as whether the test is indeed valid and reliable. That is why we included this step in the development of a test. Technology can help teachers efficiently analyze test results. Teachers can use scan sheets for student responses on select-response items and receive a printout of student results. It is critical, however, that the student results be reconnected with the intended learning outcomes in the table of specifications. Further discussion about using assessment results can be found in Chapter 6.

Conclusion: A Note about the 10 Steps

This chapter provided a step-by-step process in developing a valid and reliable test. When reading this chapter you may think to yourself, "I don't have time to follow this step-by-step process for every test that I design." The process may sound time consuming or cumbersome. However, it need not be. Most of the steps occur simultaneously, because teachers take into account these myriad factors when designing a test. Also, once teachers are aware of issues related to validity and reliability when designing a test, the process becomes second nature. We have offered many templates here in this chapter; but, as mentioned before, developing a table of specifications or analyzing data results can be done in most any format. The key here is not to keep a formal documentation of test construction, but rather to retain these ideas as the test is being constructed.

Table of Specifications for _____ **(unit of study)**

Grade _____

Content	Level of Cognitive Demand											
	Knowledge		**Comprehension**		**Application**		**Analysis**		**Synthesis**		**Evaluation**	
	Evident:	Emphasis:	Evident:	Emphasis:	Evident:	Emphasis:	Evident:	Emphasis:	Evident:	Emphasis:	Evident:	Emphasis:
	# Items:	Item Types:	# Items:	Item Types:	# Items:	Item Types:	# Items:	Item Types:	# Items:	Item Types:	# Items:	Item Types:
	Evident	Emphasis:	Evident	Emphasis:	Evident	Emphasis:	Evident	Emphasis:	Evident	Emphasis:	Evident	Emphasis:
	# Items:	Item Types:	# Items:	Item Types:	# Items:	Item Types:	# Items:	Item Types:	# Items:	Item Types:	# Items:	Item Types:
	Evident:	Emphasis:	Evident:	Emphasis:	Evident:	Emphasis:	Evident:	Emphasis:	Evident:	Emphasis:	Evident:	Emphasis:
	# Items:	Item Types:	# Items:	Item Types:	# Items:	Item Types:	# Items:	Item Types:	# Items:	Item Types:	# Items:	Item Types:
	Evident:	Emphasis:	Evident:	Emphasis:	Evident:	Emphasis:	Evident:	Emphasis:	Evident:	Emphasis:	Evident:	Emphasis:
	# Items:	Item Types:	# Items:	Item Types:	# Items:	Item Types:	# Items:	Item Types:	# Items:	Item Types:	# Items:	Item Types:

1   Bausell, C. V. (2007). *Quality counts 2007: State of the states.* Retrieved February 20, 2007, from http://www.edweek.org/media/ew/qc/2007/17sos.h26.standards.pdf

2   Porter, A. C. (2002). Measuring the content of instruction: Uses in research and practice. *Educational Researcher, 31*(7), 3–14.

3   Florida Sunshine State Standards, Mathematics Grades 3–5. Retrieved February 1, 2007, from http://www.firn.edu/doe/curric/prek12/pdf/math3.pdf

4   Bloom, B. S. (1956). *Taxonomy of educational objectives: The classification of educational goals.* New York: Longman.

5   Anderson, L. W., & Krathwol, D. R. (Eds.). (2001). *A taxonomy for learning, teaching, and assessing: A revision of Bloom's taxonomy of educational objectives.* New York: Longman.

6   Ornstein, A. C., & Hunkins, F. P. (1998). *Curriculum foundations, principles, and issues* (3rd ed.). Boston: Allyn and Bacon.

7   Bloom (1984).

8   Anderson & Krathwol (2001).

9   Blank, R. K. (2002). Using surveys of enacted curriculum to advance evaluation of instruction in relation to standards. *Peabody Journal of Education, 77*(4), 86–121.

10 Gamoran, A., Porter, A. C., Smithson, J., & White, P. A. (1997). Upgrading high school mathematics instruction: Improving learning opportunities for low-achieving, middle income youth. *Educational Evaluation and Policy Analysis, 19*(4), 325–338.

11 Florida Sunshine State Standards, Mathematics Grades 3–5. Retrieved February 1, 2007, from http://www.firn.edu/doe/curric/prek12/pdf/math3.pdf

12 Virginia Department of Education. (2002). English Standards of Learning for Virginia Public Schools. Retrieved March 12, 2008, from http://www.doc.virginia.gov/VDOE/superintendent/Sols/2002/EnglishK-12.pdf

13 California Content Standards, Grade Seven Music, Retrieved January 2, 2007 from http://www.cde.ca.gov/be/st/ss/mugrade7.asp.

14 Wisconsin Model Academic Standards, Grade Twelve Economics, Retrieved January 2, 2007 from http://dpi.wi.gov/standards/ssd/ssd12.html.

15 Nevada State Standards, Grade 5 Health, Retrieved April 8, 2008 from http://www.doe.nv.gov/standards/health_physical_ed/health/healthstandards.attachment/attachment/Health%20Standards.pdf.

16 Maryland State Voluntary Curriculum, Grade 7 Writing, Retrieved April 8, 2008 from http://mdk12.org/instruction/curriculum/reading/standard4/grade7.html.

17 Hogan, T. P. (2007). *Educational assessment: A practical introduction.* Hoboken, NJ: Wiley Jossey-Bass.

18   York County School Division. *Science Curriculum Framework.* Retrieved January 15, 2007, from http://yorkcountyschools. org/pos05/science. pdf

19   Notar, C. E., Zuelke, D. C., Wilson, J. D., & Yunker, B. D. (2004). The table of specifications: Insuring accountability in teacher made tests. *Journal of Instructional Psychology, 31*(2), *115–129.*

4

How Do I Create Good Select-Response Items?

Any teacher who has ever written items for a test will attest to the fact that writing a good question that addresses the content and level of cognitive demand can be difficult and time consuming. Any teacher who has written select-response items will also agree that writing items that are clear, concise, and free from error can be challenging. This is not to say that teachers should throw up their hands in surrender. By keeping in mind some basic rules and principles when writing select-response items, teachers can greatly reduce error in a test, thereby increasing the degree of reliability of the test, and teachers can become more proficient and efficient in writing test items that address both lower and higher cognitive levels. **Select-response items** are items that have predetermined responses from which the student may choose. Select-response items addressed in this chapter include true–false, matching, and multiple choice.

Figure 4.1. Types of Select-Response Items

Types of Select-Response Items
✓ Multiple Choice
✓ True–False
✓ Matching

Getting at higher cognitive levels with select-response items can be difficult, but not impossible. As discussed in Chapter 3, addressing appropriate cognitive levels is just as important as addressing appropriate content. An item that addresses only one of these compromises the validity of the item, and therefore the validity of the test. True–false and matching sets lend themselves to assessing lower cognitive level standards or objectives. Multiple choice items are good for assessing lower level cognitive behaviors, too; however, they are also well-suited for assessing higher level thinking, as well. One misconception regarding state assessments that mainly use multiple choice items is that these tests must be assessing only lower level learning and so teachers may think that multiple choice items they develop for their own tests can only measure lower level objectives. We hope to dispel that myth. With that said, the purpose of this chapter is to:

- ◆ explore the basic rules for writing select-response items, with a particular emphasis on writing multiple choice, and
- ◆ share principles for writing multiple choice items that address higher cognitive levels of learning.

Some Basic Rules for Writing Select-Response Items

By following some basic rules in creating select-response items, a teacher can reduce systematic error and therefore increase the reliability of individual test items. Put differently, a teacher can have more confidence in asking herself, "Did the student answer a question *correctly* because he truly *knew* the answer and nothing in the item gave the answer away? Conversely, did the student answer a question *incorrectly* because he truly did *not* know the answer and something in the item did not confuse the student to the point that, even though he knew the correct answer, he chose an incorrect answer?" By reducing the potential for error in a test question, you can have more confidence that the results of an assessment are true indications of what students *have* or *have not* learned.

In schools, students are taught test-taking skills. Open up any resource in this area and you are likely to find a set of tips such as those found in Figure 4.2.

These tips teach students how to spot systematic error and how to take advantage of random error in a test item. Although teachers have no control over random error, they can make efforts to reduce systematic error. Reducing systematic error does not *trick* students; instead, it provides students with a chance to truly share what they know and are able to do, and it provides teachers with accurate information about student achievement.

In this section, basic rules of item construction for each type of select-response item are provided. Also, for each rule a poor example that violates the rule and a better example that illustrates the rule are presented, along with a brief explanation. These rules were compiled from various assessment sources, as well as from our collective experience as teachers, instructional leaders, and item developers.[1]

Figure 4.2. Sample Test-Taking Tips

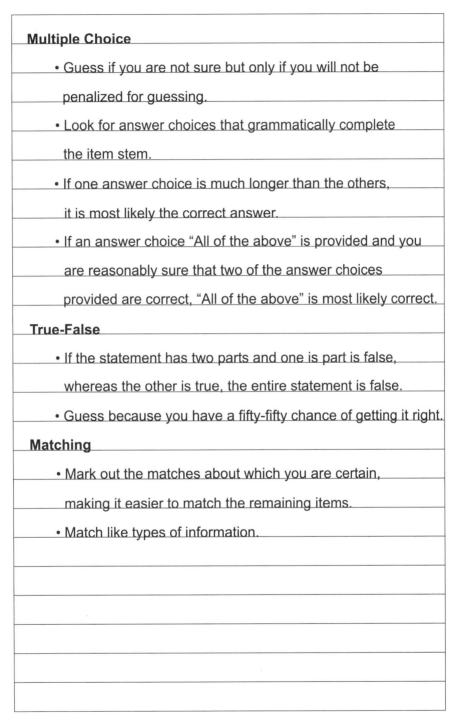

Multiple Choice

• Guess if you are not sure but only if you will not be penalized for guessing.

• Look for answer choices that grammatically complete the item stem.

• If one answer choice is much longer than the others, it is most likely the correct answer.

• If an answer choice "All of the above" is provided and you are reasonably sure that two of the answer choices provided are correct, "All of the above" is most likely correct.

True-False

• If the statement has two parts and one is part is false, whereas the other is true, the entire statement is false.

• Guess because you have a fifty-fifty chance of getting it right.

Matching

• Mark out the matches about which you are certain, making it easier to match the remaining items.

• Match like types of information.

Most of the rules described in this next section relate to the reliability of the item. Before turning our attention to this critical aspect of item construction, we must emphasize two basic rules related to validity that apply to *all* item types. First, whether you are creating a matching set, true-false, or multiple choice item, make sure that the item type is the most appropriate to use for the content and level of cognitive demand. Second, make sure that the item indeed assesses the content and the level of cognitive demand you intend. An item with a low degree of validity cannot provide useful information to you, your students, or anyone else.

Now let's take a closer look at the principles and rules that govern the three most common types of select-response items.

True-False Items

True-false items involve choosing one of two options. Therefore, the students have a 50% chance of getting it right! True-false can be used to test lower level standards but should be used sparingly and in conjunction with other types of items. Can you imagine a test that had only true-false items? The possibility of random error would be so high that you would have scant confidence in the test results. When developing true-false items, there are five rules to keep in mind. See Figure 4.3 for a quick reference list of the rules.

Figure 4.3. Summary List of True-False Item Construction Rules

True-False Item Construction Rules
Rule #1: Place only one idea in the true-false statement.
Rule #2: Make sure the statement is absolutely true or absolutely false.
Rule #3: Avoid qualifiers such as always and never.
Rule #4: Avoid opinion statements.
Rule #5: Avoid using negatives in the statement.

Rule #1: Place Only One Idea in the True-False Statement

Have you ever taken a test with true-false items and there are actually two ideas that may be true or false? What makes the situation even more complicated is when one part of the statement is true and one part is false. How confusing to students... and to teachers! Even if the student gets the item correct, the teacher may not be sure whether the student had an understanding of both ideas because they were not tested separately. So, the best option is to include only one idea in a true-false statement. Let's look at two examples in Figure 4.4.

Figure 4.4. Place Only One Idea in the True-False Statement

Poor Item: Condensation turns gases into liquids, and evaporation turns liquids into solids.
Better Item: Condensation turns gases into liquids.

In the poor item, the student must respond to two ideas related to the water cycle. What makes the situation worse is that one part of the statement is true, whereas the other is false. What is a student to do? The student who marks *false* is partially correct and the student who marks *true* is partially correct. The error in this item prevents teachers from truly knowing whether the students understand different aspects of the water cycle.

Rule #2: Make Sure the Statement Is Absolutely True or Absolutely False

This rule relates to Rule #1 in that only one idea should be present in the statement and that idea should be *absolutely* true or *absolutely* false. Consider the item previously discussed—part of the item is true and part of the item is false. Students should not be put in the position of having to decipher whether *true* would be the optimal choice or whether *false* would be the optimal choice. Let's look at two examples in Figure 4.5.

Figure 4.5. Make Sure the Statement Is Absolutely True or Absolutely False

Poor Item: Metals are made of atoms with few electrons in their outer energy level.
Better Item: Sodium is an example of an alkaline metal.

The statement in the poor example is in the grey area of decision making. The statement is true for most metals but not for all. In the better example, the statement is absolutely true. Sodium is an example of an alkali metal. If a statement is partially true and partially false, either answer could be correct, compromising the reliability of the item.

Rule #3: Avoid Absolute Qualifiers Such as *Always, Never, Sometimes,* and *Usually*

Absolute qualifiers such as *always* and *never* oftentimes give the correct answer away. Let's look at two examples from music in Figure 4.6.

Figure 4.6. Avoid Qualifiers Such as *Always* and *Never*

Poor Item:
When a sharp comes before a note, you always play the next highest key.
Better Item:
A sharp before a note indicates that the next highest key is to be played.

The poor item includes the word *always* when this qualifying term is unnecessary. This word may confuse or trick a student, and he or she may answer incorrectly or correctly based on the qualifying term rather than responding to the content contained in the statement. The better item deletes *always* since the qualifying term is unneeded.

Rule #4: Avoid Opinion Statements

Opinion statements are just that—opinions. So, how can a student respond *true* or *false* based on someone's own thoughts and beliefs? The only time when an opinion statement may be used in true-false is if the item is assessing whether students can recognize the opinions of others. Let's look at two examples in Figure 4.7.

Figure 4.7. Avoid Opinion Statements

Poor Item:
Nonviolent protest is the *best* way to bring about social change.
Better Item:
Mahatma Gandhi believed that nonviolent protest was the *best* way to bring out social change.

In the first statement students are responding to an opinion. The statement does emphasize the qualifier *best*, but a student may find the statement true or false based on her or his own opinions. The better item, however, places the opinion statement within a context. The statement does not measure whether the student agrees that nonviolent protest is the best way to bring about social change but rather the statement measures whether students know that Mahatma Gandhi believed in nonviolent protest.

Rule #5: Avoid Using Negatives in the Statement

Negatives tend to confuse students. Use negatives only if they are absolutely necessary and central to the content. Let's look at two examples in Figure 4.8.

Figure 4.8. Avoid Using Negatives in the Statement

Poor Item: Condensation does not turn gases into liquids.
Better Item: Condensation turns gases into liquids.

The poor item simply does not make sense and may be confusing to students. They may miss the *not* and read the statement as a positive. There is no compelling reason to write the item in the negative. By writing the item in the positive, the teacher can have more confidence that the item actually measures whether a student understand the process of condensation rather than whether the student was confused by the word *not*.

As stated at the beginning of this discussion of true-false items, the true-false format is essentially a selection between two possibilities. Such item types are sometimes referred to as *binary choice* item types. True-false is the most common example of a binary choice question format, but the format can also be used in other ways:

- ◆ Yes/No
- ◆ Fact/Opinion
- ◆ Supported/Unsupported

In fact, binary choice items can be used for practically any learning objective for which distinguishing between two ideas, categories, set of attributes, or the like is the intended cognitive activity. In these cases, the preceding five rules still apply.

Matching

Matching items serve a purpose of making sure that students can *recall* terms, places, people, events, ideas, and so forth. Matching sets typically measure lower levels of cognitive demand. As with true-false items, matching should be used in conjunction with other item types if other levels of cognitive behavior are identified in the learning objectives that are being assessed. However, truth is stranger than fiction and, in our experiences as teachers and working with teachers, we have indeed come across tests that include matching only.

When developing a matching set, there are a few basic rules to follow. These are summarized in Figure 4.9.

Figure 4.9. Rules for Constructing Matching Sets

Rule #1:	Use homogeneous content in a matching set.
Rule #2:	Place item to be matched on the right with the longer responses on the left.
Rule #3:	Keep the matching set short.
Rule #4:	Use an uneven number of items to match or allow responses to be used more than once.
Rule #5:	Order items in a logical manner.

Instead of a matching set to serve as an example for each rule, Figures 4.10 and 4.11 are used to discuss how each rule is important. These matching sets focus on identifying the contributions of various Americans, symbols of the United States, and United States holidays.

Figure 4.10. Matching Set

Poor Matching Set

Directions: Match the following items to the appropriate response.

1. George Washington
2. Martin Luther King, Jr.
3. Abraham Lincoln
4. Veterans Day
5. Memorial Day
6. Washington Monument
7. Thurgood Marshall
8. Independence Day
9. Thomas Jefferson
10. Jackie Robinson
11. Statue of Liberty
12. Rosa Parks
13. American flag
14. bald eagle
15. George Washington Carver

a. first African-American Supreme Court Justice
b. has fifty stars on it
c. the day we celebrate United States independence from Great Britain
d. first African-American baseball player to play in the major leagues
e. first president of the United States
f. the day we give thanks to men and women who have served in the armed forces
g. given to the United States by France
h. civil rights leader
i. refused to give up her seat on a bus
j. located in Washington, DC
k. founded the Tuskegee Institute
l. president during the Civil War
m. national emblem of the United States
n. the third president of the United States
o. the day we remember those who have died fighting war

Figure 4.11. Better Matching Set

Better Matching Set

Directions: Write the letter of the person described by each statement. You may use each person more than once.

1. First African-American Supreme Court Justice
2. Refused to give up a seat to a white man on a bus
3. First African-American baseball player to play in the major leagues
4. Founder of the Tuskegee Institute
5. Led a march on Washington to bring attention to civil rights
6. Led court case *Brown v. Board of Education* to end segregation
7. Found uses for agricultural products such as peanuts and sweet potatoes
8. Received the Nobel Peace prize for work in civil rights

a. George Washington Carver
b. Martin Luther King, Jr.
c. Thurgood Marshall
d. Rosa Parks
e. Jackie Robinson

Rule #1: Use Like Content in a Matching Set

The material within a matching set should be homogeneous in nature. In the poor matching set example (Figure 4.10), students are matching three different types of information—famous Americans, American symbols, and American holidays. For example, in matching any of the people, the student can dismiss many of the responses as they do not refer to people. Furthermore, the student can identify Rosa Parks fairly easily as the only response that refers to a female, thereby finding the match for letter *i.*

In the better matching set (Figure 4.11), only historical figures are used and even that set is further narrowed by focusing on African-Americans who influenced Civil Rights.

Rule #2: Place Items to Be Matched on the Right With Descriptions on the Left

Take a look at the poor matching set. When a student reads, "George Washington," she must read through every response to find a match. This involves a great deal of re-reading and is an inefficient use of time. The better matching set places the response on the left hand side. So, when a student reads, "First African-American Supreme Court Justice," she needs only to skim the names to find a match.

Rule #3: Keep the List Short

Matching sets should be kept to a minimum. The maximum number of items in a matching set should be ten for older students and even less for younger students.[2] Notice in the poor matching set that students have 15 items to match and, in the better matching set, they have eight items to match. By using like content, the matching set is kept at a minimum.

Rule #4: Provide an *Uneven* Number of Responses to Match

In the poor matching set, there are 15 items to match 15 responses. Therefore, when students get to the end of the matching set, the last few items are usually given to them merely by process of elimination. What's more, if a student answers incorrectly for one match, he or she will automatically miss a second one as well. In other words, it's not possible to just miss one when the matching sets are even. Matching sets should either have more responses than students can use, or the items should be able to be used more than once. In the better matching set, the directions indicate that each person may be used more than once. Hence, the process of elimination is eliminated! However, make sure that the directions clearly indicate that items may be used more than once or that some responses may not be used at all.

Rule #5: Order Responses in a Logical Manner

The items to be matched in a set should be in some type of logical order: numerical order, alphabetical order, short to long, and so on. In the poor item set, the items to be matched are not placed in any type of logical order and so are quite confusing. Students must switch their thinking from events to holidays to famous Americans. In the better item set, the items to be matched are homogeneous in nature, and they are placed in alphabetical order by last name.

Multiple Choice Items

Multiple choice items are the most commonly used item types on state assessments. In fact, 49 out of the 50 states and the District of Columbia use multiple choice items to assess student performance, and two states use *only* multiple choice items.[3] Multiple choice is also an icon of classroom-based testing, with this type of item noted in early American education.[4] For this reason, we devote a great deal of attention to the development of multiple choice items that are both valid and reliable.

Throughout this section we use some terms to describe parts of a multiple choice item. Take a look at Figure 4.12 as a visual referent for these key terms.

Figure 4.12. Multiple Choice Terms

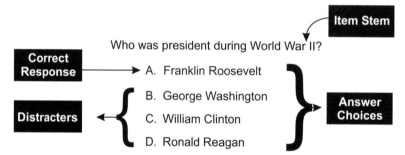

The rules for developing reliable multiple choice items are divided into two sections. The first section contains rules for developing the item stem, and the second section contains rules for developing the answer choices. Figure 4.13 provides a summary of the rules for constructing multiple choice items.

Figure 4.13. Rules for Constructing Multiple Choice Items

Stem

Rule #1: Make the problem clear to the student in the item stem.

Rule #2: State the item stem in the positive whenever possible.

Rule #3: Make sure the item stem does not give away the correct answer.

Rule #4: Emphasize qualifiers such as *most likely* and *best* in the item stem.

Answer Choices

Rule #5: Make sure the answer choices are plausible.

Rule #6: Develop answer choices that are parallel in grammar and in length.

Rule #7: Avoid using "All of the above" and "None of the above."

Rule #8: Place the answer choices in a logical order.

Rule #9: Avoid clues in the answer choices that give away the correct response.

Rule #10: Make sure that the correct response is the only correct response.

Item Stem

The item stem is essentially the question. It serves the purpose of orienting the student to what is being asked. There are two basic formats for a multiple choice item stem:

1. *Explicit question,* with answer choices from which to select
2. *Sentence completion,* with grammatically consistent words, phrases, numbers, or symbols from which to select.

Regardless of the format used, the following four rules apply to constructing the item stem of a multiple choice question.

Rule #1: Make the Problem Clear to the Student in the Item Stem

The problem should be in the item stem and not in the answer choices. This rule relates to providing enough information in the item stem to give the student an indication of what is being asked. It also relates to removing unnecessary or confusing information from the question. Let's look at two examples in Figure 4.14.

Figure 4.14. Make the Problem Clear to the Student

Poor Item	Better Item
Antigens A. Attack memory cells B. Attack Killer T cells C. Attack pathogens D. Attack helper T cells	Which of these do antigens attack? A. Pathogens B. Helper T cells C. Killer T cells D. Memory cells

In the poor example, not enough information is provided. The student does not know what information he or she should think about related to antigens. The problem is made clear in the answer choices, rather than the item stem. The question is asking what antigens attack. In the better item, the item stem clearly indicates that this is the focus of the item. The better item still has a concern, however, because only one of the answer choices is a one-word choice whereas the others are made up of two words and each has the word "cells" in it.

Rule #2: State the Item Stem in the Positive Whenever Possible

As former classroom teachers and test item developers, we recall becoming extremely frustrated at our inability to think of plausible distracters when creating multiple choice questions. So, we found ourselves sometimes converting the item stem to a negative. This conversion was sometimes a cop-out. However, there are instances when a negative in the item stem is necessary. In science class we teach lab rules in the negative: Do not put your hand over the open flame of a Bunsen burner. You may chuckle when reading this, but how could this lab rule be stated in a positive manner? The rule could be, "Stay away from flames"; but in using the Bunsen burner, the student must be near the flame. For some instructional objectives, assessing student knowledge using an item stated in the negative may be very appropriate. However, for most of what is taught this is *not* the case. Negatives can confuse students. Also, students may not catch the negative when reading the item. Therefore, for those times when you do use a negative, be sure to emphasize it in some way, such as by using **bold-face,** *italicized,* or <u>underlined</u> type. Let's look at two examples in Figure 4.15.

Figure 4.15. If Possible,
State the Item Stem in the Positive

Poor Item	Better Item
Which of these is not a reason why President Roosevelt decided not to involve the United States in World War II until the bombing of Pearl Harbor?	Which of these *best* describes why the United States became involved militarily in World War II?
A. The United States was upset with Great Britain over the sinking of merchant ships. B. The United States was involved in another war at the time. C. The United States was already allied with Germany at the time of Pearl Harbor. D. The United States had not been attacked directly until Pearl Harbor.	A. The United States was directly attacked. B. Great Britain asked for assistance against German submarines. C. French resistance needed military arms after Germany invaded. D. The United States was obligated to become involved by its membership in NATO.

The poor example of the item stem is confusing as students have to sort through two negatives in the question. The better test item eliminates the negative.

Rule #3: Make Sure the Item Stem
Does Not Give Away the Correct Answer

Sometimes the item stem itself can inadvertently give away the correct answer. For example, one of the most well-known foibles is to end the item stem with the article *an* when only one answer choice begins with a vowel. However, there are other ways that item stems can give away the correct answer. Consider the two examples in Figure 4.16.

Figure 4.16. Make Sure the Item Stem
Does Not Give Away the Correct Answer

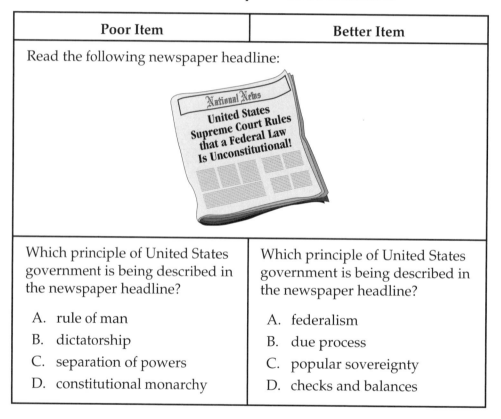

Poor Item	Better Item
Read the following newspaper headline: *National News — United States Supreme Court Rules that a Federal Law Is Unconstitutional!*	
Which principle of United States government is being described in the newspaper headline? A. rule of man B. dictatorship C. separation of powers D. constitutional monarchy	Which principle of United States government is being described in the newspaper headline? A. federalism B. due process C. popular sovereignty D. checks and balances

If the student knows his Constitutional principles, he does not need the newspaper headline to get the poor item correct. Because the correct response is *checks and balances*, the phrase *principle of United States government* provides a clue to the correct answer. In the first example, the correct response is the only one that is a principle of United States government. Therefore, a teacher does not know if the student selected the response merely because he knew separation of powers is a principle of government or if he interpreted the headline correctly. In the better example, each answer choice is a principle of the United States government; therefore, the student would need to know each constitutional principle to answer the question correctly.

Rule #4: Emphasize Qualifiers Such as *Most Likely* or *Best* Used in the Item Stem

Qualifiers in the stem such as *most likely*, *best*, or *least likely*, are terms that the student needs to take into account when reading the item. Let's take a look at two examples.

**Figure 4.17. Emphasize Qualifiers
Such as *Most Likely* and *Best* in the Item Stem**

Poor Item	Better Item
Matthew was paid $20 for mowing his neighbor's lawn. If he spends $5.50 on a movie rental, $6.75 on a pizza, and $2.00 for a soda, which is closest to the amount he will have left? A. $ 5.00 B. $ 0 C. $14.00 D. $ 9.00	Matthew was paid $20 for mowing his neighbor's lawn. If he spends $5.50 on a movie rental, $6.75 on a pizza, and $2.00 for a soda, which is *closest* to the amount he will have left? A. $14.00 B. $ 9.00 C. $ 5.00 D. $ 0

In this item the word *closest* is a qualifier that lets students know what is being asked. They are simply being asked to estimate the amount leftover, not the exact amount left over. In the poor item, the word *closest* does not stand out to the test-taker at all. A student may miss the word and become confused because the exact amount is not available in the answer choices. In the better item, the word *closest* is italicized and the student is clued in to estimation of the amount.

Answer Choices

The second critical part of creating valid and reliable multiple choice items is to develop quality answer choices. Many times developing the answer choices, particularly the distracters, can be a great challenge and cause much angst. On state assessments, students are typically provided with four answer choices. In developing your own tests, you should have no less than three and no more than five answer choices. The next set of rules relate specifically to addressing sources of systematic error in answer choices.

Rule #5: Make Sure the Answer Choices Are Plausible

Have you ever wanted to bring a little levity to a testing situation? Some of the answer choices may be silly or so ridiculous that students break into a smile when they read it. This isn't such a bad thing when a teacher has rapport with the students in her class, but the teacher must be aware that there is a principle of item construction that will be affected. Providing silly or ridiculous answer choices that are not plausible compromises the reliability of items because students can easily dismiss these answer choices.

Mathematics teachers have been writing plausible answer choices for years. A student may add instead of subtract, for example, and an answer choice would be available for this common error. An advantage of having plausible answer choices based on common errors in logic or procedure is that the students' choosing of the incorrect answer choice gives teachers some insight about areas in which students may struggle. Let's look at two examples in Figure 4.18.

Figure 4.18. Make Sure Answer Choices Are Plausible

Poor Item	Better Item
Who was president during World War II? A. Franklin Roosevelt B. George Washington C. George W. Bush D. Jesse James	Who was president during World War II? A. Dwight Eisenhower B. Lyndon Johnson C. Franklin Roosevelt D. Woodrow Wilson

This item assesses student learning at the recall level. Students must merely know who the president was during World War II to associate specific people with specific events. In the poor item, the possible answer choices are far removed from the event and the answer choice *Jesse James* is quite silly (especially because he isn't even a past president). In the better item, the answer choices focus on presidents during the twentieth century and those who were president during wartime. The answer choices are much more plausible.

Rule #6: Make Sure Answer Choices Are Parallel in Grammar and Length

Answer choices should begin in the same way and should be about the same length. If the correct response is a one-word noun, the rest of the answer choices should be one-word nouns. If the correct response begins with a verb, the distracters should also begin with verbs. If one answer choice is much longer than the others, it may provide a clue to the correct response. If one answer choice must be long, and one must be short, a good option would be to have two short answer choices and two long answer choices. Let's look at two examples in Figure 4.19.

Figure 4.19. Develop Answer Choices That Are Parallel in Grammar and Length

Poor Item	Better Item
In English class, Cynthia must write a descriptive essay about the person she admires the most. She wants to write about her father. Which of these would be the *best* way she could begin to write her essay?	
A. Look through old pictures of her and her father	A. By looking at her baby pictures
B. She could call her best friend to talk about him.	B. By asking her father to come to her class
C. By making a list of activities she has done with her father.	C. By calling her best friend to talk about her father
D. Asking her father to come to her class	D. By listing all of the things he has done for her and others

In the poor item, the answer choices are grammatically inconsistent and confusing. In the better item, each answer choice begins in the same fashion.

Rule #7: Avoid Using *All of the Above* or *None of the Above*

Have you ever written a multiple choice item with four answer choices and you have no problem developing the correct response and two really great distracters but the final distracter is just not there? You may have put in the old faithfuls, *all of the above* or *none of the above,* as the last answer choice.

We have seen many assessments developed by teachers in which *all of the above* or *none of the above* is always the last answer choice and is used with frequency. We have also observed that these are oftentimes *not* the correct choices for the questions in which they are used. In other words, they are not plausible distractors. Let's look at two examples in Figure 4.20.

Figure 4.20. Avoid Using *All of the Above* and *None of the Above*

Poor Item	Better Item
Which of these should be used to measure in millimeters? A. A yard stick B. A metric ruler C. A digital scale D. None of the above	Which of these should be used to measure in millimeters? A. A yard stick B. A metric ruler C. A digital scale D. A graduated cylinder

In the poor item the last answer choice is *None of the above* when this answer choice is unnecessary. The item focuses on measurement and measuring in metric units. Another plausible answer choice is the *graduated cylinder* because it is a tool for measuring and can measure in metric units. The graduated cylinder measures volume rather than length but does offer an attractive option.

It is important to add a caveat about this rule; namely, there is an exception to it! In some cases, *None of the above* and *All of the above* can be plausible options. If they are used throughout a test as answer choices and they are indeed sometimes the correct answer, they can be appropriate to use as choices.

Rule #8: Place Answer Choices in a Logical Order

Answer choices should be placed in some type of order, and ordering systems should be consistent throughout any given test. Here are a few guidelines:

 ◆ Place numbers in numerical order
 ◆ Place one-word answer choices in alphabetical order
 ◆ Order sentences from shortest to longest

One reason for placing answer choices in a logical order is to ensure random placement of the correct response. When developing multiple choice items, you might begin with the correct response as the first choice, as usually the correct response is the simplest to develop. If the correct response is left as the first answer choice on each item, students pick up the pattern. Figure 4.21 provides examples to consider. In the poor item, the answer choices are not in any logical order and the correct response is first. In the better item, the answer choices are ordered from the least to greatest. The ordering of the answer choices in the poor item can be confusing for the student.

Figure 4.21. Place the Answer Choices in a Logical Order

Poor Item	Better Item
What is the next number in the pattern? 54, 53, 52, 51, 50, 49, _____ A. 48 B. 50 C. 47 D. 59	What is the next number in the pattern? 54, 53, 52, 51, 50, 49, _____ A. 47 B. 48 C. 49 D. 50

Rule #9: Avoid Clues in the Answer Choices That Give Away the Correct Response

Sometimes a clue to the correct response can be found in the answer choices. The correct response may contain a similar term that is used in the item stem or the answer choice may be the only choice that grammatically completes the item stem. Be sure to review the correct response to make sure that it does not give away the correct answer. Let's take a look at two examples in Figure 4.22.

Figure 4.22. Avoid Clues in the Answer Choices That Give Away The Correct Response

Poor Item	Better Item
Which of the following revolutions resulted in increased business by speeding travel? A. industrial B. technology C. textile D. transportation	Which of the following *best* describes a result of the transportation revolution in the 1800s? A. Suburban areas grew. B. Demands for slave labor decreased. C. Manufacturing and production increased. D. People relied less on mass transportation.

In the poor item, a word in the item stem gives a clue as to the correct answer. The words *travel* and *transportation* are clearly linked. In the better item, the student must know a result of the transportation revolution, and there are no clues in the item stem that give away the correct answer.

Rule #10: Make Sure the Correct Response Is the Only Correct Response

This may sound like a silly rule, but it is paramount to reliability. The correct response should, in fact, be accurate and should be the *only* possible correct response. No other answer choice presents an equal or better option. Look at the items in Figure 4.22 that were just discussed with the previous rule. In the poor item, there is more than one correct response. One could argue that *industrial* is also a correct response because the industrial revolution made it possible for railroads to be built. The better item includes only one correct response.

A Final Consideration: Bias

Each student comes into the classroom with a wide range of experiences and exposure to ideas, words, and terms germane to specific languages, cultures, societies, and socioeconomic backgrounds. When writing any type of select-response item, review the item and ask the following question: Are there any words or phrases used in the item that would put a student with limited English proficiency or a student with different sociocultural experiences at a disadvantage? Consider the example in Figure 4.23.

Figure 4.23. Avoiding Bias in an Item

Poor Item	Better Item
Chicago Bears : football :: _____ : baseball	large : big :: triumph : _____
A. Anaheim Angels	A. loss
B. Los Angeles Galaxy	B. rule
C. Sacramento Kings	C. small
D. Tampa Bay Buccaneers	D. success

The two items presented in the examples are analogies. A purpose of analogies is to determine a student's ability to understand the relationship between concepts and ideas. Therefore, a student must have experiences with the concepts or ideas to understand the relationships. In the poor item, the student's ability to understand the relationship presented is influenced by her exposure to sports teams, the examples here being teams in the United States. This content is not critical to any subject area, places the student at a disadvantage, and calls into question the *construct validity* of the item. (See the discussion of *construct validity* in Chapter 2; in short, the intent of the question is not to assess knowledge of sports teams.) In the better item, the terms are not tied to popular culture but rather focus on commonly used vocabulary terms.

Bias can have insidious effects on assessments. By definition, we are oftentimes *unaware* of our own biases. What's more, it is quite difficult to account for the individual experiences and backgrounds of all of the students in our classrooms. The caution we raise here is that teachers must attempt to be aware of biases that may influence assessment results and then control for the influence of those possible biases. After all, reducing the influence of bias is a means of increasing the reliability and the validity of an assessment.

Some Principles for Tapping Higher Cognitive Levels of Learning through Multiple Choice Items

As discussed in Chapter 3, state standards and instructional objectives require that students engage with content at the higher cognitive levels of learning. Select-response item types such as true-false and matching are typically not conducive to assessing these higher cognitive levels. A common misconception regarding multiple choice items is that only lower cognitive levels can be assessed. However, multiple choice items can assess content at both lower and higher cognitive levels. Therefore, this section addresses only this type of select-response item.

To make the point that multiple choice questions can assess higher cognitive levels, consider the following item in Figure 4.24.

Figure 4.24. Sample Multiple Choice Item that Taps Higher-Order Thinking

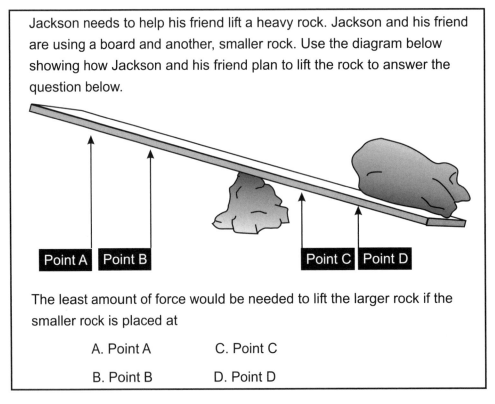

Jackson needs to help his friend lift a heavy rock. Jackson and his friend are using a board and another, smaller rock. Use the diagram below showing how Jackson and his friend plan to lift the rock to answer the question below.

Point A Point B   Point C Point D

The least amount of force would be needed to lift the larger rock if the smaller rock is placed at

A. Point A   C. Point C

B. Point B   D. Point D

In this test item, students must interpret not only the stimulus material provided in the diagram but the students must also interpret each of the answer choices. The students must *know* and *comprehend* simple machines, force, the role of a fulcrum, levers and a host of other terminology and concepts related to simple machines. The students must *apply* what they have learned about simple machines, *analyze* and *interpret* the diagram, and then make a judgment regarding the best possible answer. The student must also *analyze* the answer choices. This item represents one item similar to state assessments in one subject area. However, reviewing state assessments reveals similar types of items that do, indeed, assess higher cognitive levels of thinking. Therefore, teachers must not only *teach* at higher cognitive levels, but must also *assess* at higher cognitive levels.

There is one disclaimer that we must make at this time. It is difficult for a multiple choice item to assess at the levels of *evaluation* or *synthesis*. By their very nature, multiple choice items are forced choice, meaning the students cannot offer an answer that is not provided. Evaluation and synthesis require that students construct their own meaning, rather than reasoning an already conceived answer. A multiple choice item could provide various bits of information for students to synthesize, but the construction of meaning for the student is limited to the answer choices. So, our intent here is to show how multiple choice items can tap cognitive levels of *comprehension, application,* and *analysis.*

In this section we explore five principles for writing multiple choice items at higher cognitive levels (Figure 4.25). For each principle, a brief description is followed by a poor item and a better item that illustrates the principle. An explanation of what makes the better item *better* follows each. We use the term *better* rather than *best* because we recognize that all items have some error. It is virtually impossible to write an item that is free from systematic error. However, steps are taken to reduce that error by following the basic guidelines set forth in the first part of the chapter.

Figure 4.25. Five Principles for Writing Higher Cognitive Level Multiple Choice Items

Principle #1: Refine your understanding of *content* and *cognitive levels*

Principle #2: Introduce novelty

Principle #3: Focus on complex content

Principle #4: Use an extended prompt

Principle #5: Provide stimulus material

Principle #1: Refine Your Understanding of Content and Cognitive Levels

Creating multiple choice questions that tap higher-order thinking requires that the question creator have a clear understanding of the *content* being assessed and intended levels of student *cognition*. As a reminder from previous discussion in Chapter 3, content can be stated explicitly in the objectives or standards, and content may also be implicit or conditional. Cognitive levels may be lower levels, such as recall, or higher levels, such as analysis or evaluation. For example, *recalling* types of poetry and *analyzing* poetry for figurative language require different cognitive behaviors, although the content may be similar. Let's review examples in Figure 4.26.

Figure 4.26. Refine Your Understanding of Content and Level of Cognitive Demand

State Standard
New York State Standards of Learning—Intermediate Health Education Analyze the multiple influences which affect health decisions and behaviors.

Poor Item:	Better Item:
What is used to measure weight? A. a scale B. a thermometer C. a blood pressure cuff D. a stethoscope	Anna goes to the movies with her friends and some of them are smoking cigarettes and so are the actors in the movie. Her parents have discussed the dangers of smoking with her. Her best friend offers her a cigarette, but Anna tells her friend that she does not want a cigarette. Which of these *most likely* had the greatest influence on Anna's decision? A. the actors B. her parents C. her best friend D. her peer group

The state standard focuses on the *analysis* level of cognitive demand, and the content relates to the factors that influence health decisions. The poor item misses the mark on both content and level of cognitive demand. The poor item focuses on measuring weight, which can give an indication of health but does not address the standard. What's more, the item is written at the *recall* or *knowledge* level.

In the better item, students are presented with a scenario and asked to determine which of the people presented had the greatest influence on Anna's decision not to smoke a cigarette. This item requires analysis, and it also requires students to think about the influences on Anna's health decision. Therefore, it addresses both the content and the level of cognitive demand contained within the standard.

This first principle serves as a foundation for each of the other principles. To truly teach and assess a standard or an instructional objective, teachers must have an understanding of the content and level of cognitive demand contained within the standard. This exercise is similar to Step 1: Unpacking Your Standards already discussed in Chapter 3. The type of thinking required influences the type of item that is written.

Principle #2: Introduce Novelty

Novelty is an essential component of creating higher level multiple choice questions. Novelty requires students to apply what they have learned. Merely replicating a task completed in class usually reaches knowledge and comprehension levels of Bloom's Taxonomy, even if the task seems difficult on the surface. In social studies, for example, students may analyze primary source documents to explore the foundations of Constitutional principles. If a multiple choice question asks students to identify a Constitutional principle based on an excerpt from a document discussed in class, the question may function as a recall question. However, if students are asked to identify a Constitutional principle based on an excerpt they have not seen, the question presents a novel situation. Let's review the example in Figure 4.27.

Figure 4.27. Introduce Novelty

State Standard

Texas Essential Knowledge and Skills (TEKS) for English Language Arts and Reading, Grade 8
Reading/text structure/literary concepts. The student analyzes the characteristics of various types of texts (genres). The student is expected to… recognize and interpret literary devices such as flashback, foreshadowing, and **symbolism**.

Poor Item:	Better Item:
At the end of the novel *The Pearl* by John Steinbeck, the pearl has become a symbol of _____. A. humans' struggle against and eventual triumph over the forces of nature B. humans' ability to survive great emotional pain, although not unchanged C. humans' capacity for love even in the face of death D. humans' triumph over evil through strength	By the end of the novel *The Pearl* by John Steinbeck, the pearl has become a symbol of humans' ability to survive great emotional pain, although not unchanged. What is *most likely* symbolized when Kino throws the pearl into the sea at the end of the story? A. Kino's envy of the upper class B. Kino's hatred of Coyotito's killers C. Kino's acceptance of his status in life D. Kino's willingness to sacrifice for a better future

The content in this state standard from Texas focuses on literary devices used in various types of genres. The standard is written at a higher cognitive level as students must *analyze, recognize,* and *interpret* various genres for symbolism. The identification and interpretation of symbolism in fiction involves higher-order cognitive behaviors. One may well imagine most middle school teachers leading their students in engaging discussions about symbolism in a variety of pieces of fiction. However, if a teacher helps students identify and interpret a symbol during class discussions, and then, on an assessment, merely asks students to *recall* the symbol that was identified and discussed in class, the teacher has inadvertently assessed a lower-order thinking skill. By introducing *novelty*—or asking students to interpret a symbol in a way that has *not* yet been discussed or addressed directly in class—teachers can have students engage in higher-order thinking.

Presumably, the poor sample item represents recall of a complex symbol. In the better example, the teacher has not discussed the final symbolism of the pearl in class, thereby reserving the interpretation of the symbol in the final scene for the students. This principle reinforces the crucial link between instruction and assessment. Instruction must be examined to determine whether an item does or does *not* present a novel situation.

Principle #3: Focus on Complex Content

The content of questions can be *simple* or *complex*. Simple content is either one dimensional or consists of relatively few components. Complex content is made up of multiple factors or components. For example, a list of dates of major battles during the Civil War is relatively simple material—it may not be particularly easy to memorize, but the content is rather simple—dates and names. However, an explanation of the interrelated events leading up to any one of these battles could be quite complex. Simple content is often appropriately measured at lower levels of cognitive behavior (e.g., recall or comprehension), whereas complex content often can be appropriately assessed at higher levels of cognition (e.g., analysis or evaluation). Let's review examples based on third-grade science (Figure 4.28).

Figure 4.28. Focus on Complex Content

State Standard

Virginia Standard of Learning—Grade 3 Science

The student will investigate and understand the water cycle and its relationship to life on Earth. Key concepts include... processes involved in the water cycle (evaporation, condensation, precipitation)

Poor Item:	**Better Item:**
When water evaporates it turns into a _____. A. liquid B. solid C. gas D. solution	On a very hot day, there is a brief rain shower, followed by the return of the sun. The small puddles of water on the streets will *most likely* turn into _____. A. gases B. liquids C. solids D. solutions

The water cycle is the content contained within this state standard from Virginia. More specifically, students should know the process of the water cycle, including evaporation, condensation, and precipitation. The verbs *investigate* and *understand* indicate that students should engage with this content at higher cognitive levels.

In the poor sample item, the one-dimensional nature of the question amounts to *recall* thinking for students, because they are essentially asked to provide a definition of evaporation. In the better sample item, students must *comprehend* and *analyze* the interrelationship among the states of matter and the environmental context to respond to the question correctly. Knowing the definition of evaporation is essential, and the poor item may be clearly legitimate if the purpose of the item is to assess at the knowledge level. However, to accurately address the standard presented in the example, understanding of the water cycle process is key, of which evaporation is a part.

Principle #4: Use an Extended Prompt

Extended prompts provide students with some background information needed to answer the question and usually involve two or three sentences of text. They introduce complexity by providing contextual information.

However, when using extended prompts, be sure to think about whether the student could answer the question *without* the information. If so, the information is unnecessary and the question may actually focus on knowledge and comprehension, rather than higher level thinking. Also, make sure that the extended prompt does not provide the correct answer. If so, then the question really measures the students' comprehension of the contextual information, rather than the content being assessed (Figure 4.29).

Figure 4.29. Use an Extended Prompt

State Standard
Wisconsin Model Academic Standards—Grade 12 Social Sciences Explain the United States' relationship to other nations and its role in international organizations, such as the United Nations, North Atlantic Treaty Organization, World Bank, International Monetary Fund, and North American Free Trade Agreement.

Poor Item:	**Better Item:**
The war-torn region of Bosnia needed help after a civil war erupted. They were without food, medicine, and shelter. The Red Cross sent teams of volunteers to address the issues. The United States supports the Red Cross monetarily. Based on this description, the purpose of the Red Cross is to:	A member country in the North Atlantic Treaty Organization (NATO) is invaded by a country that is not a member of NATO. The United States sends troops to the country attacked. In this situation, the United States took the action described because member countries of NATO _____.
A. create trade agreements B. provide humanitarian assistance C. provide loans for the country to rebuild D. form military alliances with governments	A. invade threatening countries B. defend other member countries C. support invasions by member countries D. provide monetary support to member countries

Many state standards in social studies focus on the importance of international organizations. Wisconsin is no different. The state of Wisconsin expects that by the time a student graduates from high school, he or she will have studied the United States' role in international organizations. The state of Wisconsin expects students to be able to *explain* the relationships among these entities, not to merely have knowledge of the purposes of the international organizations.

In the poor item, a student does not need the extended prompt to answer the question. A student only needs to know the purpose of the Red Cross. The poor item does not describe the United States' relationship to the Red Cross. The information provided in the extended prompt is ancillary and fails to address the standard directly.

In the better item, a situation is described and the question focuses on the United States' responsibility as a member of the North Atlantic Treaty Organization (NATO). The extended prompt is needed to answer the question because answer D could be a correct answer choice. However, based on the description, the correct answer choice is B. Therefore, students must *analyze* the situation and call on their own understanding of the role of the United States in NATO.

Principle #5: Engage With Stimulus Material

Stimulus material is similar to an extended prompt in that students must use information given to answer the question. Stimulus material includes diagrams, charts, maps, pictures, excerpts from documents, and so forth. Cautions regarding extended prompts also apply to using stimulus material. The stimulus material should be necessary to answer the question, and the stimulus material should not explicitly provide the correct answer. Instead, stimulus material should require students to *interpret* the information or data presented. Oftentimes, stimulus material can be used as the basis of several test questions. Let's review two examples in Figure 4.30.

Patterning begins early in a child's education. In the state of Florida, by the time students complete the third grade, they should know what a numerical or geometric pattern is. The state of Florida also expects that students be able to have not only *knowledge* of these patterns, but they also must be able to *extend* and *create* patterns, indicating higher cognitive behaviors.

The stimulus material in Figure 4.30 requires students to examine a chart with a sequence of numbers. In the poor item, students are merely reading the chart. The question focuses on *comprehension* but not on extending or creating numerical patterns. The poor item even fails to hit the content standard, because what is being measured is really the skill of chart interpretation.

In the better item, students must *analyze* the pattern and *extend* the number sequence. To extend the number pattern, students must analyze the incremental increases in savings to determine the pattern. The better item more closely aligns with the intended cognitive level of the standard as well as the content, including patterns and number sequences.

Stimulus material offers a way for students to interact with content in a novel way, thereby increasing the level of cognitive behaviors being assessed. By including stimulus material, teachers can determine whether a student can *apply* or *analyze*. Stimulus material requires students to integrate existing knowledge with a new situation.

Figure 4.30. Engage With Stimulus Material

State Standard
Florida Sunshine State Standards—Grade 3 Mathematics
The student describes, extends, and creates numerical and geometric patterns through models (for example, concrete objects, drawings, simple number sequences).

Manuel wants to save his money. Each week he puts more money into his piggy bank.

Week	Money Put Into Bank
1	$0.25
2	$0.50
3	$0.75
4	$1.00
5	?

Poor Item:	Better Item:
How much money did Manuel save in Week 1?	If his savings pattern continues, how much money will Manuel put into his bank in Week 5?
A. $ 0.25	A. $1.10
B. $ 0.50	B. $1.25
C. $ 0.75	C. $1.50
D. $ 1.00	D. $1.75

Developing Valid and Reliable Select-Response Items: A Science and an Art

The science behind creating items that indeed test what they intend to assess and are free from systematic error are laid out in this chapter and in Chapter 3. You have read about 10 steps to creating a valid test by assessing both the content and level of cognitive demand. You have also examined rules related to constructing selected-response items that serve to decrease systematic error. These rules are fairly cut and dry—the science of creating valid and reliable select-response items. However, creating the items also involves art—wordsmithing to get the right wording of the answer choices or choosing just the right stimulus material for students to interact with on a test.

This chapter focused on reliability as it relates to reducing systematic error by carefully developing select-response items. This chapter also examined how to increase the degree of validity by ensuring that test items assess the range of cognitive levels found in standards and instructional objectives. By following the basic rules set forth in item construction and the principles of assessing higher level standards, teachers can increase the degree to which their assessments are both valid and reliable.

1   Gronlund, N. E. (2006). *Assessment of student achievement* (8th ed.). Boston: Pearson; Hogan, T. P. (2007). *Educational assessment: A practical introduction.* Hoboken, NJ: Wiley Jossey-Bass; Popham, W. J. (2002). *Classroom assessment: What teachers need to know* (3rd ed.). Boston: Allyn and Bacon; Stiggins, R. J. (2005). *Student involved assessment for learning* (4th ed.). Upper Saddle River, NJ: Merrill; Taylor, C. S., & Nolen, S. B. (2005). *Classroom assessment: Supporting teaching and learning in real classrooms.* Upper Saddle River, NJ: Pearson.

2   Gronlund (2006); Hogan (2007).

3   Bausell, C. V. (2007). State of the states. *Quality Counts 2007: From cradle to grave.* Retrieved May 25, 2007, from http://www.edweek. org/media/ew/qc/2007/17sos.h26.assessments.pdf

4   Shepard, L. A. (2000). *The role of classroom assessment in teaching and learning.* Report published for the Center for Study of Evaluation (CSE Technical Report #517). Retrieved May 5, 2007, from http://www.cse. ucla.edu/Re

5

How Do I Create Good Supply-Response Items?

Supply-response items allow teachers to assess a range of cognitive levels, depending on the type of supply-response item and the complexity of the item. **Supply-response items** are items for which the student must provide the answer. In this chapter we focus on three specific types of supply-response items: fill-in-the-blank or completion, short answer, and essay. These types of items can be used on paper-and-pencil tests and are a mainstay of item types for teacher-made tests. Other supply-response assessment items include performance assessments, projects, and original creations. However, these types of assessments do not lend themselves to paper-pencil tests and are usually conducted as part of an overall assessment plan that may include paper-and-pencil tests *and* projects, performance assessments, or original creations.

The first part of the chapter addresses writing supply-response items that are free from systematic error. These rules are a compilation of our review of assessment experts in the field as well as our own experiences as teachers, instructional leaders, state assessment developers, and, currently, professors.[1]

The second part of the chapter focuses on writing supply-response items that assess higher cognitive levels. The final part of the chapter is devoted to developing scoring rubrics for short answer and essay items, as a scoring rubric is key to addressing validity and reliability.

Some Basic Rules for Writing Supply-Response Items

The purpose of the following basic rules in creating supply-response items is to reduce systematic error and to increase the reliability of these items. The challenge in creating a valid and reliable supply-response item is to develop the item in such a way so that:

- ◆ the item assesses what you as the teacher intend for it to assess

- the student can respond in a way that truly demonstrates what she has, or has not, learned
- the item does not give away the correct response
- the item does not *prevent* a student from providing an appropriate response

For each type of supply-response item discussed, a rule is provided along with a poor example, a better example, and an explanation of how the examples demonstrate the rule.

Fill-in-the-Blank or Completion Items

Fill-in-the-blank or completion items are useful for assessing lower cognitive levels such as *knowledge* and *comprehension*. They can help eliminate guessing because a student must know the correct answer and cannot choose from a supplied list of possible responses. Fill-in-the-blank items are also fairly easy to grade and allow for an efficient use of test time. Some tests use word banks with completion items. Do not confuse these types of items with supply-response items; they are more akin to matching sets because students *choose* from the possible options offered in a word bank. If using fill-in-the-blank with a word bank, refer to the guidelines to creating matching sets discussed in Chapter 4. As for conventional fill-in-the-blank items that do *not* use word banks, there are some basic rules that will help you create and use such test item types in valid and reliable ways (Figure 5.1).

Figure 5.1. Rules for Constructing
Fill-in-the-Blank or Completion Items

> Rule #1: Position the blank at the end of the statement.
>
> Rule #2: Limit the number of blanks in a statement.
>
> Rule #3: Keep blanks the same length.

Rule #1: Position Blanks at the End of the Statement

The position of the blank at the end of the completion statement provides the student with an understanding of what is being asked at the beginning. By way of contrast, if the blank is positioned at the beginning of the statement, the student will most likely have to read the statement again, thereby reducing the efficiency of the item. Let's look at two examples (Figure 5.2).

Figure 5.2. Position Blank at the End of the Statement

Poor Item:
A _____ converts kinetic energy into electrical energy.

Better Item:
Kinetic energy is converted into electrical energy by a(n) _____.

In the poor item, the student is not quite sure what is being asked until the very end of the statement. Then the student has to go back and reread the item to figure out the correct response. In the better item, the student has an understanding of the focus of the item by the time he or she reads the entire item.

Rule #2: Limit the Number of Blanks

Have you ever seen a fill-in-the-blank item that is missing so many words that the student would have to be a mind reader to respond correctly? We certainly have. This introduces error into the item by not giving the student enough information to be able to knowledgeably respond. Let's look at two examples (Figure 5.3).

Figure 5.3. Limit the Number of Blanks

Poor Item:
A _____ sends _____ of electrical current through _____.

Better Item:
Pulses of electrical current are sent through wire by a(n) _____.

In the poor item, the student has a slim chance of getting the correct answers. The only detail provided in the statement is "electrical current." How would a student know that the item is trying to elicit whether the student knows how a telegraph works? In the better item, enough information is provided that the student knows what is being asked and has an opportunity to demonstrate that he knows how a telegraph works, if indeed he does.

Rule #3: Keep All Blank Spaces the Same Length

When reading this rule, you can probably imagine why this would be important. If some blanks are longer than others, the student may be given a clue that the correct response is a longer word or phrase, whereas shorter blanks may mean that the correct response is a shorter word or phrase. Let's look at the following examples (Figure 5.4).

Figure 5.4. Keep Blanks the Same Length

Poor Items: The first major agreement between United States officials and Plains Indians was called the _____. The President can pardon illegal acts by granting _____.
Better Items: The first major agreement between United States officials and Plains Indians was called the _____. The President can pardon illegal acts by granting _____.

In the poor items, the student knows that the correct response in the first item is longer than the correct response in the second item. In the better items, each blank is equal in length, thereby reducing the possibility of a student gaining a clue to the correct answer based only on the format of the test item, rather than eliciting the answer from the student's understanding of the material. Of course, there is one important caution to keep in mind: If you intend for students to write their answers in the blanks that you provide, the blanks should be long enough to accommodate the expected answers.

Short Answer Items

Short answer items are useful in assessing a range of cognitive levels. They require a bit more than a single word or a phrase as an answer, such as in a completion item; but short-answer items are not quite the extensive response required in an essay item. As of 2007, 33 states used short answer on state assessments.[2] A benefit of short answer items is that they can assess content that cannot be easily assessed on a select-response or fill-in-the-blank item. For example, a teacher may develop a simple addition problem with two-digit numbers in a multiple choice format. However, if the teacher wants to know whether students can carry over in adding two-digit numbers, it would be more useful for students to show their work. Then, the teacher can assess whether the students can actually carry out this computation. There are three simple rules when constructing a short-answer item. These are listed in Figure 5.5.

Figure 5.5. Rules for Constructing Short Answer Items

Rule #1:	Make the question and the nature of the response clear to the student.
Rule #2:	Develop a scoring rubric to accompany each item.
Rule #3:	Provide adequate space for a response.

Rule #1: Make the Question and the Nature of the Response Clear to the Student

A question that is unclear to students is plagued by systematic error. The student may give a response that makes perfect sense and may even be correct but is not what the teacher intended. One way to make the question clear is to think about what the correct response would be and build the question around the correct response. It is also important to let students know what you expect in the response. Do you expect complete sentences? Do you expect to see a mathematical computation? Let's look at two examples (Figure 5.6).

Figure 5.6. Make the Question Clear to the Student

Poor Item:

Discuss synthesis reaction and decomposition reaction.

Better Item:

Provide a difference between synthesis reaction and decomposition reaction.

In the poor item, students are given the direction to discuss the two concepts of synthesis and decomposition reaction when the item really is meant to assess the *differences* between the two; so why not phrase the question that way? In the better item, students know that they need to think about the differences between synthesis and decomposition reaction and provide one difference. Students can more clearly understand the intent of the question and therefore have a better opportunity to respond.

Rule #2: Develop a Scoring Rubric to Accompany Each Short Answer Item

Without a scoring rubric for a short answer item, the grading of student responses may become too subjective and, therefore, unreliable. Broadly, a **scoring rubric** is a description of the nature of an acceptable response. When scoring is unreliable, neither teachers nor students can draw appropriate inferences about learning; that is, the item becomes less valid. A scoring rubric can improve the validity of the item, because it is in the scoring rubric that a teacher delineates the content and level of cognitive demand that are being assessed. For this rule, we provide a poor example and a better example (Figure 5.7); however, later in the chapter we discuss the creation of rubrics more extensively.

Figure 5.7. Develop a Scoring Rubric to Accompany Each Item

Poor Item With Rubric:
Jamal made two cookies for each of his kids. He has three kids. How many cookies did Jamal make? Show your work.
Scoring Rubric: 2 total points for correct response and work shown.
Better Item With Rubric:
Jamal made two cookies for each of his kids. He has three kids. How many cookies did Jamal make? Show how you got your answer using words, numbers, or pictures.
Better Scoring Rubric:
2 points: Correct number of cookies and accurate depiction of problem using words, numbers, or pictures.
1 point: Correct number of cookies; lacks depiction of problem using words, numbers, or pictures.
0 points: Incorrect response to number of cookies or no response.

In a manner of speaking, the rubric tells the story of what the student is required to do. In the poor item, the students have a clear problem to solve, and the directions indicate that the students should show their work. The rubric in the poor item is not a rubric at all, it is a simple listing of the number of points for the item. It seems that this short answer question is an all-or-nothing assessment item. In the better item, students are provided with more information about how to show their work, and the rubric indicates exactly how the two points are awarded.

Rule #3: Provide Adequate Space for the Response

Adequate space for the response should be provided to students. Younger students may need more space than older students because they are developing their handwriting skills. Teachers should also consider whether students would be better served by responding in a lined response space rather than a blank response space. The response space provided for each short answer item may need to be equal in size so as not to provide a clue that one short answer item requires more information than another short answer item.

Essays

Essay items provide teachers with the opportunities to assess higher cognitive levels. Essays may require students to analyze policies for similarities and differences, synthesize information to formulate a novel understanding, or evaluate the veracity of an argument. An essay takes much more time for students to complete and for teachers to grade. However, essay items allow teachers to assess higher cognitive levels as well as a greater depth of content.

Essay items are used extensively in state assessments, particularly when evaluating writing ability. As of 2007, all but 2 states used essays or extended constructed responses in English, and 26 used extended constructed responses in other subject areas.[3] Clearly, these states recognize that to validly assess whether a student can write an essay, a set of multiple choice items asking students to critique a written paragraph falls short. To assess whether students can write an essay, students must actually write one!

The rules that apply to short answer items also apply to essay or extended constructed response items, but there are additional rules to consider, as well. These rules are listed in Figure 5.8. We must note, however, that one essential and hopefully obvious guideline regarding essay items is that they must be developmentally appropriate, which includes an understanding that teachers provide enough time for students to respond to the essay prompt and that the point value associated with the item is appropriate.

Figure 5.8. Rules for Constructing Essay Items

Rule #1:	Make the question and the nature of the response clear to the student.
Rule #2:	Avoid options within the question.
Rule #3:	Develop a scoring rubric to accompany each essay item.

Rule #1: Make the Question and the Nature of the Response Clear to the Student

This rule is similar in nature to Rule #1 for short answer items. In order for a student to provide an appropriate response, the essay prompt must be written so as to elicit an appropriate response. One concern we often hear with this rule is, "Aren't we then just giving the answers to the students?" The answer is no. An essay item that is too broadly written, or too narrowly written, puts the student in an unfair situation. If it is too broadly written, students apply their own interpretation to the question, which may not be what the item intended. If the item is too narrowly written, the student may focus in a rote manner only on what the item asked rather than employing higher-order thinking and developing an insightful response. One way to address this situation is to draft an outline of an exemplary response first, and then craft the essay prompt itself. Let's look at two examples of essay prompts (Figure 5.9).

Figure 5.9. Make the Question and the Nature of the Response Clear to the Student

Poor Item:

Discuss how African-Americans worked to gain civil rights in the 1950s and 1960s.

Better Item:

In a five paragraph essay, describe how African-Americans worked to gain civil rights in the 1950s and 1960s in the following ways: socially, politically, and economically. Include specific historical events in your response to support your ideas.

In the poor item, the students have a wide range of what to discuss in their responses. However, the intent of the item is to assess whether students understand the ways in which African-Americans gained civil rights and the specific historical events associated with the civil rights movement. The better item reflects this intent. This question requires higher-level thinking as students must analyze the events of the civil rights movement and place these events into three distinct categories. The better item also places some conditions on the students' responses. The response must be in the form of a five-paragraph essay and the response must include historical events. These provide clear criteria for students constructing responses as well as teachers assessing the students' essays.

Rule #2: Avoid Options Within the Question

Have you ever taken a test with essay items in which you have a choice of answering three of the five (or some optional number) essays provided? You probably wiped your forehead in relief as you could more easily answer some items than others, so you wrote the ones for which you had the most confidence. The two prompts you did not answer were questions for which you may have not had the foggiest understanding or were a bit shakier on your details. What a relief!

In education, we talk a great deal about providing choice to students. Although this can allow for differentiation, it poses a problem for assessing student understanding of important learning objectives. If students have a choice among multiple essay prompts, each of which assesses different content and possibly at different cognitive levels of demand, how can teachers draw inferences about student learning regarding the content of the essays that were *not answered*? It is extremely important for teachers to understand the purpose of the essay item or essay items if there are more than one. Figure 5.10 shows an example.

Figure 5.10. Avoid Options Within the Question

Poor Item:

Choose any one of the following three essays. Your response will be based on the story *The Diary of Anne Frank.*

> Option 1: Describe the central conflicts in the book, both internal and external, and how the conflicts were resolved, if they were resolved.
>
> Option 2: Choose two of the characters in the book and describe how these characters are developed and how they change throughout the book.
>
> Option 3: Describe how imagery is used in the book.

Better Item:

In class, we read *The Diary of Anne Frank.* Throughout the book, Anne describes her family members and the conflicts they faced both with the outside world and among themselves. Using the essay model we have discussed in class, describe the following:

> 1. Two conflicts, either external and/or internal, faced by Anne and her family
> 2. How the character traits of the family members influenced how they dealt with the conflicts

Use events from the story to support your ideas.

In the poor item, students can choose from one of three options. The first option focuses on conflict, the second option focuses on character development, and the third option focuses on the use of imagery. First, these types of items may not be the most appropriate given the nature of the story, *The Diary of Anne Frank.* Second, each essay item assesses something different; so the teacher would have different assessment information for each student. In the better item, the question is more focused and also more appropriate for the novel being studied. The question focuses on integrating both conflict *and* character by intertwining the two. Therefore, the essay assesses a broader range of content and each student writes to the same question, allowing the teacher to make comparisons among student performance and interpret student responses in light of the learning objectives, which are represented on the teacher's table of specifications for the test. Because the better item drops the question related to imagery, the teacher would have to assess that content through some other means.

Rule #3: Develop a Scoring Rubric to Accompany Each Essay Item

An essay *without* a scoring rubric leads to serious reliability concerns. How will the essay be graded? Will the same criteria be applied to all essays? Will the essay be graded based on essential content and skills, not just grammar and composition? These questions must be answered prior to the administration of the test. The rubric helps to delineate exactly what teachers expect in the essay response, thereby clarifying the essay question. Let's look at examples in Figure 5.11.

Figure 5.11. Develop a Scoring Rubric to Accompany Each Essay Item

Item:
In class, we read *The Diary of Anne Frank.* Throughout the story, Anne describes her family members and the conflicts they faced both with the outside world and among themselves. Using the essay model we have discussed in class, describe the following: 1. Two conflicts, either external and/or internal, faced by Anne and her family   2. How the character traits of the family members influenced how they dealt with the conflicts   Use events from the story to support your ideas.

Poor Scoring Rubric:
20 points: 10 for each conflict

Better Scoring Rubric:	
Exemplary (20 points):	The response indicates a clear and insightful level of understanding of the conflicts faced by Anne and her family and how the character traits of the family members influenced how they dealt with the conflicts. Events from the story directly support the description of the conflict and family member character traits. The essay is well-written, convincing, and follows the format discussed in class. The essay is generally free from grammatical errors.

Proficient (15 points):	The response indicates an understanding of the conflicts faced by Anne and her family and how the character traits of the family members influenced how they dealt with the conflicts. Events chosen from the book support the description of the conflict and family member character traits, but events that were more directly relevant would have made the essay stronger. The essay is clear and develops a rational position, essentially following the format discussed in class. The essay contains some grammatical errors.
Developing/ Needs Improvement (10 points):	The response indicates a limited understanding of the conflicts faced by Anne and her family and how the character traits of the family members influenced how they dealt with the conflicts. Events chosen from the book offer weak support of the description of the conflict and family member character traits. The essay lacks elements discussed in class and contains numerous grammatical errors.
Unsatisfactory (5 points):	The response indicates a weak or inaccurate under-standing of the conflicts faced by Anne and her family and how the character traits of the family members influenced how they dealt with the conflicts. Events do not support the description or are not provided. The essay lacks elements discussed in class and contains numerous grammatical errors.

No response (0 points)

The rubric examples provided in Figure 5.11 are based on the essay from Figure 5.10. The poor rubric in Figure 5.11 is limited and leaves a great deal of room for interpretation. The teacher may also intend to grade on essay format and grammar, but these elements are not taken into account in the poor rubric. In the better rubric, the number of points awarded is clearly delineated and the teacher knows what she will be looking for when she grades each essay. Essentially she is looking for four items:

1. Description of the conflicts and how Anne's family dealt with the conflicts

2. Support from the story

3. Correct application of elements of a well-written essay

4. Correct use of grammar

This rubric provides the teacher with a clear direction in grading, while also providing the student with a clear sense of the expectations for a response. Rubrics should be shared with students so that they are aware of the expectations.

A Final Consideration: Bias

Students have varying experiences based on myriad factors. These factors include the students' native language, developmental level, and exposure to concepts and ideas at home, in museums, and other cultural institutions. Sometimes terms or phrases may be used in a supply-response item that places some students at a disadvantage because of their background. When writing a supply-response item, a teacher must review the item to make sure that the language and terms are critical to the content being assessed and do not unfairly penalize students who do not have experiences with the terms or phrases but could demonstrate their understanding of the instructional objective nonetheless (Figure 5.12).

Figure 5.12. Reviewing Items for Bias

Directions: Correct this sentence.
have you ever read time magazine

Student response:
Have you ever had time to read a magazine?

The example shows a supply-response item in which students must correct grammatical errors in a sentence. The student response shows how the student corrected the sentence. The item was intended to measure grammar use, specifically capitalization and punctuation. In particular, the item was measuring whether students know that proper nouns should be capitalized. The student response indicates that the student probably did not know that *Time* was the name of a magazine because he or she was not exposed to it; so the student changed the sentence so that it made sense to him or her. Based on how the student corrected the sentence, the teacher does not know whether the student knows that proper nouns should be capitalized. Because of bias, the item inadvertently introduced error into the assessment; therefore, the reliability and validity of the item are weakened.

Principles for Tapping Higher Cognitive Levels of Learning Through Short Answer and Essay Items

In Chapter 4, we provided five principles for developing multiple choice items to assess higher cognitive levels. Typically, supply-response items, particularly essays, have been used to assess levels of *application, analysis, synthesis,* and *evaluation.* So why even address this issue in this chapter? In our experience, short answer and essay questions in some instances may look on the surface as if they are assessing higher cognitive levels; but, in reality, they are assessing *recall* or *knowledge.* The same principles that we discussed with multiple choice items can be applied to supply-response items, specifically short answer and essay items. In this section, we briefly review each principle and provide an example of a poor item and a better item to illustrate the principle. For a more thorough description of the principle, please refer back to Chapter 4.

Principle #1: Refine Your Understanding of Content and Level of Cognitive Demand

This principle essentially relates to the validity of an item. Does the item indeed address the content and the level of cognitive demand contained within a state standard or an instructional objective? Perhaps the item addresses the content but not at the level of cognitive demand required. Let's review two examples in Figure 5.13.

Figure 5.13. Refine Your Understanding of Content and Level of Cognitive Demand

State Standard
Nevada Standards—Advanced Music
Students listen to, analyze, and describe music… analyze examples of a varied repertoire of music representing diverse genres and cultures by describing the uses of the elements of music and expressive devices.

Poor Item:	Better Item:
Explain the devices used in calypso music.	Listen to the following two pieces of music for elements of music that represent a culture.
	Describe the expressive devices used in the music pieces and how they represent their respective cultures.
	[Students listen to the two pieces of music].

This standard from the state of Nevada focuses on the *use* of expressive devices in various cultures and the *analysis* of music across cultures. Students must be able to listen to musical pieces and to explain how certain expressive devices are indicative of a culture. In the poor item, students are merely asked to explain what devices are used in calypso music. They do not have to listen to calypso music to identify the devices. In the better item, the students must listen to two pieces of music, identify the expressive devices used, and explain how these devices shed light on the culture from which the music came. The students are analyzing two pieces of music rather than one. The poor item misses the mark on the level of cognitive demand and on the content.

Principle #2: Introduce Novelty

Novelty involves students' application of what they have learned to a new situation or thinking about information in a different way. Students must have requisite knowledge and skills to answer the question. Let's consider a high school social studies class in which the students are comparing and contrasting the North and South prior to the Civil War. The teacher teaches the students about the North and South, and the students prepare an extensive graphic organizer detailing the similarities and differences. Figure 5.14 shows two essays built around this content.

Figure 5.14. Introduce Novelty

State Standard	
North Carolina Standard Course of Study—Grade 11 Social Studies (American History)	
The learner will analyze the issues that led to the Civil War, the effects of the war, and the impact of Reconstruction on the nation.	
Poor Item:	**Better Item:**
Describe the similarities and differences between the North and South prior to the Civil War. Use historical facts to support your response.	Examine the following broadside from the Civil War. [insert example of broadside] In a well-written essay, explain the following: <ul><li>the issue that is the focus of the broadside</li><li>the views of the North and South regarding this issue</li><li>the effects of the issue on the Civil War</li><li>the resolution of this issue after the Civil War</li></ul>Use historical facts to support your response.

The North Carolina state standard here focuses on the issues leading to the Civil War, events, and outcomes during Reconstruction. In many history classes, the similarities and differences between the North and South are discussed at length; and, in this particular scenario, the students completed an extensive graphic organizer in class. Because novelty is not introduced in the item, the poor item amounts only to *recall*. On the surface it looks like it is an analysis question. But when instruction is taken into account, the true nature of the cognitive level is revealed. Sure, the students must formulate the response; however, they are merely writing what they have already discussed in class.

In the better item, the students encounter a broadside which exemplifies an issue related to the Civil War. They must *interpret* the broadside, *analyze* the broadside for the issue, and then *synthesize* the broadside with the similarities and differences that contributed to the Civil War. The broadside ensures that the students have a level of understanding of the issue and cognitively wrestle with their understanding and the novel prompt . . . a far stretch from recall.

Principle #3: Focus on Complex Content

Content can be viewed as simplistic or complex. For example, describing conflict in an essay may be more simplistic than applying the character traits of those within the novel and how the characters dealt with conflict. Short answer and essay items that address more complex content tend to assess higher level thinking. Consider the examples in Figure 5.15.

Figure 5.15. Focus on Complex Content

State Standard Texas Essential Knowledge and Skills—English IV
Reading/literary concepts. The student analyzes literary elements for their contributions to meaning in literary texts. The student is expected to: . . . compare and contrast elements of texts such as themes, conflicts, and allusions both within and across texts.

Poor Item:	**Better Item:**
Describe a conflict in *Life of Pi* by Yann Martel. Provide evidence from the text to defend your description.	The conflict between an idealistic and a pragmatic response to life is a recurrent theme in *Life of Pi* by Yann Martel. Write an essay in which you analyze the reasons for the conflict between these two ways of responding to life's events and compare their respective effects on one idealistic character and one more realistic character. Provide evidence from the story to defend your analysis.

This item was built around the Texas Essential Knowledge and Skills for high school English. The state of Texas expects students to be able to *identify* conflict as well as *analyze* conflicts for similarities and differences. In the poor item, students must only identify a conflict in the novel *Life of Pi*. This is a simplistic view of the standard and only scratches surface of the intent of the curricular objective.

In the better item, the student must not only identify conflicts but must do so for two different types of characters, an idealistic one and a realistic one. The student must then compare the conflict's effect on the characters, thereby tapping into *analytical thinking*. In fact, students even must first *evaluate* the characters to determine whether they are idealistic or realistic. This essay item more closely addresses the complexity of the standard.

Principle #4: Use an Extended Prompt

An extended prompt provides students with some background information. The students must then link this information with what they already know to formulate their responses. A caution when using extended prompts: The information provided should not explicitly give students the answer and should be necessary to answer the question. Let's look at an example in Figure 5.16.

Figure 5.16. Use an Extended Prompt

State Standard
Washington State Grade Level Expectations—Grade 4 Science[4]
The student will know the processes that change the surface of the Earth... identify and describe how weathering and/or erosion changes the surface of the Earth.

Poor Item:	Better Item:
The process of water carrying soil from the plastic boxes into the clear pans is called erosion. Erosion can be caused by more than just water flowing. Describe the process of erosion and explain a cause.	The process of water carrying soil from the plastic boxes into the clear pans is called erosion. Erosion can be caused by more than just water flowing. Describe a cause of erosion other than water flowing. In your description, be sure to: • identify another cause of erosion • describe how and where this other cause of erosion would occur Use words, labeled diagrams, and/or labeled pictures in your answer.

The state of Washington includes short answer items on its assessments. In this case, students must supply a response to indicate that they understand and can describe the process and causes of erosion. In the poor item, the student is merely restating the information provided in the extended prompt. This item is a reading comprehension item rather than a science item, compromising the construct validity of the item. (Revisit Chapter 2 for an explanation of construct validity.)

In the better item, the process of erosion is briefly described. Students are then asked to extend beyond the prompt provided and articulate another cause of erosion, while also describing how this cause makes erosion occur. Therefore, they are applying the concept of erosion to a new situation. The extended prompt provides enough information to interpret but does not provide the explicit answer to the item.

Principle #5: Provide Stimulus Material

Stimulus material is similar to the extended prompt in that students must interact with the information to formulate a response. The stimulus material should be necessary to respond to the short answer or essay item but should not explicitly provide clues to the answers for the students. The two examples provided in Figure 5.17 show how stimulus material can be used to raise the cognitive level of an item.

Figure 5.17. Engage With Stimulus Material

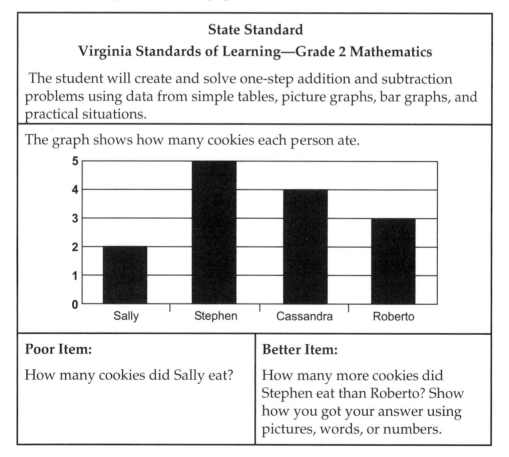

State Standard
Virginia Standards of Learning—Grade 2 Mathematics
The student will create and solve one-step addition and subtraction problems using data from simple tables, picture graphs, bar graphs, and practical situations.

The graph shows how many cookies each person ate.

Poor Item:	Better Item:
How many cookies did Sally eat?	How many more cookies did Stephen eat than Roberto? Show how you got your answer using pictures, words, or numbers.

The state standard focuses on the student's ability to create and solve addition and subtraction problems. The stimulus material provided sets the stage for students to demonstrate their abilities in this area. In the poor item, the students are merely reading the chart. But—make no mistake—reading a chart for a second grader is difficult. Therefore, interpretation is involved. However, the poor item does not really get at the standard and, in fact, fails to measure whether students can use the information in the chart to add and subtract. In the better item, the students use the information to create a subtraction problem, and then they must show their work. The teacher can adequately measure whether students can interpret the chart, create a problem, and solve it, indicating cognitive levels of *application* and *analysis*.

Developing Rubrics for Scoring Short Answer and Essay Items

A rubric is essentially the scoring criteria for an item. Select-response items are simpler and more objective to score. The student must choose from one of the answer choices provided, and the teacher grades accordingly. Fill-in-the-blank or completion items are also easier to score, because the answers provided are limited and typically involve little interpretation. Short answer and essay items are more open to interpretation and are more difficult to score. This need not be the case. Simply by articulating essential criteria, scoring an essay or short answer item becomes a more objective process, rather than wholly subjective. We do not assert, however, that applying a rubric eliminates subjectivity. It does not. Indeed, the creation and use of scoring rubrics require considerable professional judgment and subject-area expertise. Even so, when teachers grade a short answer or essay item without a rubric, scoring the response is more susceptible to *uninformed subjectivity*, *inconsistency*, and *error*, each of which diminishes the reliability and therefore the validity of the item.

Types of Scoring Rubrics

Rubrics vary in types and sophistication. Some rubrics may take a few minutes to construct and others may take much longer, depending upon the content and the level of cognitive demand of the learning objectives being assessed. The three types of rubrics that are used most often when grading supply-response items are a *checklist*, a *holistic rubric*, and an *analytical rubric*. Each type of rubric is appropriate in varying circumstances, depending on the type of item and level of information teachers need to assess student understanding. Each type is briefly explained following and an example is provided.

Checklist

A **checklist** is simply that: a list of behaviors or look-fors in an item response. Checklists are useful for a quick grading of a response. Checklists focus on certain behaviors that are associated with a task. What the checklist does *not* provide is any degree of how well the items on the checklist were performed. Teachers are simply looking to see that the content and/or behaviors are present.

With some content and skills, varying degrees of knowledge or ability may not be appropriate. For example, it would be difficult to define degrees of whether a student can perform a simple computational task. Teachers may want to see certain work shown, but varying degrees of completion are not appropriate in this instance. We recommend checklists as a possible use in evaluating responses to short answer items rather than more complex test items, such as essays. Essay items require a more complex response and thus the checklist is less appropriate. Figure 5.18 shows an example of a checklist that could be used to rate a student's response to the better item in Figure 5.17.

Figure 5.18. Example of a Checklist

☐ The student used pictures, words, or numbers to show the answer. (1 point)

☐ The pictures, words, or numbers portrayed the problem accurately. (2 points)

☐ The correct answer was provided. (2 points)

The checklist provided delineates the task to be completed. Notice that points are awarded for each item in the checklist, making this a five-point question. The first item in the checklist focuses on whether students can use pictures, words, or phrases to depict a problem, an important skill to learn. The next two items focus on accuracy, another critical consideration. So, if a student attempts to show her work using pictures but misses the mark, the student still receives one point.

Holistic Rubric

A holistic rubric is a valuable tool and one that is used by many states to assess student performance on state standardized tests. A **holistic rubric** provides a defined level of expected performance on a supply-type item that is applied to a student's overall performance but is not indicative of specific components of the performance. For example, the state of Florida uses holistic rubrics to assess student performance in reading, mathematics, science, and writing. Holistic rubrics typically involve levels of performance, ranging from a 2 to a 6. The number is associated with a description of the response. The scorer must use the levels to rate the response. A student's response may not fall into more than one category. The better rubric in Figure 5.11 provides an example of a holistic rubric. Notice that the levels of performance are described as *exemplary, proficient, developing/needs improvement,* and *unsatisfactory.* Each level also has a point value associated with it.

The holistic rubric is useful for both short-answer items and for essay items. It provides teachers with criteria to use for grading the item and gives a sense of the entire response, rather than individual pieces of the response as in the checklist. It also accounts for varying degrees of responses. The holistic rubric, however, does not provide ratings on various processes that may be involved in one item. This type of rubric is called an *analytical rubric.*

Analytical Rubric

The analytical rubric is reserved for the more complex tasks that may involve different processes or skills. An **analytical rubric** is a scoring key that provides information regarding performance in each of the component parts of the task, making it useful for diagnosing strengths and weaknesses. Students gain more information regarding their performance, and teachers gain more information regarding a student's level of performance and, therefore, further instruction that may be needed. Developing and applying an analytical rubric can be time consuming for teachers, but the information the rubric yields can be very valuable. Figure 5.19 provides an example of a rubric that might be used in a writing class. The analytical rubric is not for every type of item. A simple short answer item may require only a checklist, but a more involved task may involve a breakdown of the task for both the teacher and the student.

Figure 5.19. Example of an Analytical Rubric Used for Writing

	1	2	3	4
Composition	The response lacks significant features of composition.	The response indicates lack of several features, indicating significant weakness in the composing.	The response adheres to most of the features for composing, but struggles with consistency.	The response consistently adheres to the features for composing, with possible minor errors.
Written Expression	The response lacks significant features of written expression.	The response indicates lack of several features, indicating significant weakness in written expression.	The response adheres to most of the features for written expression, but struggles with consistency.	The response consistently adheres to the features for written expression, with possible minor errors.
Usage and Mechanics	The response lacks significant features related to usage and mechanics.	The response indicates lack of several features, indicating significant weakness in usage and mechanics.	The response adheres to most of the features for usage and mechanics, but struggles with consistency.	The response consistently adheres to the features for usage and mechanics, with possible minor errors.

The analytical rubric breaks writing into three component parts: composing, written expression, and mechanics and usage. Students may perform at the highest level in the first two areas, but at a 2 in the mechanics and usage. The student and the teacher then know that the student has the ability to write well but needs to work on grammar.

Guidelines for Developing a Scoring Rubric

A scoring rubric, whether it be a checklist, a holistic rubric, or an analytical rubric, must be developed deliberately and with careful thought. Here we provide seven guidelines for developing a rubric to score a short answer item or a complex essay item.

1. *Unpack the standard or the objective that the item and the rubric will assess.* This guideline is critical. The rubric must be aligned with both the learning objective and the item that is developed. This step—as with all test items—is your first step in ensuring the all-important attribute of *validity*.

2. *Write the short answer or essay item.* The item itself provides the starting point for the development of the checklist or rubric. Teachers must know what they are going to assess before they can develop criteria to assess it.

3. *Decide on the most appropriate type of scoring rubric.* The type of scoring rubric is dependent on the item type and the complexity of the item. The type of scoring rubric chosen is also dependent on the intended uses of the assessment results. For example, if teachers desire diagnostic information on the students' abilities to apply the skill of comparing and contrasting, an analytical rubric may be more appropriate.

4. *Design the scoring rubric.* The scoring rubric should be designed based on the type of rubric and on the item itself. Design elements of each type of rubric discussed are provided in Figure 5.20.

5. *Review the item again for alignment between the learning objective, the item, and the scoring rubric.* After developing the rubric, always look at the item again to make sure that the rubric indeed measures a student's response and to ensure that the item is written in such a way that elicits a correct response.

6. *Apply the rubric after administering the assessment.* It is our experience that applying a rubric provides a great deal of information regarding the reliability of the rubric. You may find that the rubric is not quite clear or that some of the elements unintentionally

overlap. After applying the rubric, it can be refined for the next use.

7. *Analyze the results.* The results of the rubric provide valuable information regarding student performance and the adequacy of instruction. Checklists may provide information regarding specific elements with which students have difficulty. The holistic rubric provides an overall picture of student performance on a task. The analytical rubric allows the student and teacher to diagnose specific strengths and weaknesses, in varying degrees.

These seven guidelines provide an outline of how to go about developing a scoring rubric. Just as with a table of specifications, a rubric need not be a neat, word-processed checklist or chart. It can be written out on a sheet of paper or sketched out on a napkin, for that matter! However, it is only fair to the students that they know how the short answer item or essay item is scored. The scoring rubric should be shared with students (but, hopefully, not on a napkin). Now that we have devoted attention to *developing* a rubric, we now turn to *applying* the rubric.

Figure 5.20. Design Tips for Developing Different Types of Scoring Rubrics

Checklist
- ☑ List the critical elements, facts, or procedures that must be in the response.
- ☑ Assign point values to the critical elements, facts, or procedures.

Holistic Rubric
- ☑ Decide on the number of levels of performance.
- ☑ Describe responses associated with each level of performance.
- ☑ Assign point values to each level of performance.

Analytical Rubric
- ☑ Decide on the number of levels of performance.
- ☑ Define critical elements of the task.
- ☑ Describe the anticipated response for each element at each level of performance.
- ☑ Assign point values to each level of performance.

Tips for Applying a Rubric

Following clear guidelines in developing a rubric ensures that the short answer or essay item measures what it is intended to measure and that criteria are appropriate for scoring the item. Just as important is the actual application of the rubric. The rubric you develop may have a high degree of validity in that it is aligned with both the objective and the essay item, but it may be applied in such a way that its reliability is compromised. Here are a few tips to consider as you apply rubrics to student work. Each tip provides a teacher scenario and then a discussion of the importance of the tip.

Tip #1: Score Responses Anonymously

Allen teaches eighth-grade English. The students have been working on how to write persuasive essays while reading a novel in class. The students took a test on the novel, which included a persuasive essay item based on the novel. Allen is now scoring the essays using a rubric developed by his state to prepare students for the state writing assessment. When he gets to Malachi's essay, Allen is pleased with what he is reading. Malachi always performs well in class and is a conscientious, hard-working student. When Allen gets to Erica's essay, he knows what he is going to find even before he reads the essay. Erica rarely turns in homework and her essays are usually incomplete. However, this time her essay is complete; and, in fact, her essay is just about on par with Malachi's.

All teachers are human. We develop perceptions of people based on past experiences. In Allen's case, he was expecting the *good* in Malachi's essay and he was looking for the *bad* in Erica's to confirm his perceptions. If Allen had scored the essays without knowing the identity of the essay writer in advance, his bias would have been negated. Bias can even enter into the application of a rubric. By scoring student work anonymously (that is, not knowing the students' identities while scoring), bias is limited; consequently, the reliability and validity of the assessment item is improved.

Tip #2: Review Scored Responses for Consistency in Scoring

Rhoda teaches advanced placement (AP) American history and administers essays that are comparable to essays that students may encounter on the AP exam. It takes her approximately 30 minutes to grade each essay, so the process is long. She grades some in the morning, some in the afternoon, and some in the evening. One evening she picks up an essay to grade, not realizing she has already graded the essay earlier in the day because she records comments on a separate piece of paper first. When she figures out her mistake, she finds that the score she had assigned to the student the second time was different from the first time. She decides that she needs to go back and spot check other essays.

Everyone has a different time of the day in which they are more productive and simply more in tune. Teachers are no different. Moods can influence how student responses are viewed. One way to keep yourself objective is to go back and spot-check items that you have already scored to see if you still agree with the rating. This is called *intra-rater reliability* (discussed in Chapter 2). Rhoda has a problem with intra-rater reliability, which she found out when she inadvertently scored a paper differently the second time around.

Tip #3: Have Someone Else Score Student Responses Using the Scoring Rubric

Keisha works in a middle school that emphasizes writing across the curriculum. She teaches science and has been using writing both in instruction and in assessment of student work. She recently administered a test, on which the last question was an essay item. She used the writing rubric adopted by the school to score the responses. Keisha was grading the essays in the teacher's lounge and was having difficulty scoring one student's essay. Another science teacher, Stacy, happened to be in the lounge and they began talking about the rubric. They decided that they would choose a random number of each other's students to go behind and check each others' scoring of student responses.

Sometimes the application of a rubric can be a daunting process, especially if the rubric is externally imposed, as in the case described in the preceding scenario. The situation described relates to *inter-rater reliability* (discussed in Chapter 2). Keisha is concerned with inter-rater reliability because she is not sure that she is applying the rubric correctly and would feel better if someone else scored some of her students' work independently. Then, she could compare scores to make sure that she is on target with the rubric.

Tip #4: Score Each Item With Rubric for All Students Before Moving onto the Next Item

Lucia teaches fifth-grade language arts and uses paper-and-pencil tests to assess students' understanding of various novels and the application of various literary devices found in the novels. On her tests she uses short answer and essay items. For a long time, Lucia graded each student's test various literary devices found in the novels. On her tests she uses short answer and essay items. For a long time, Lucia graded each student's test completely and then moved onto the next student's test. She went to a workshop on using scoring rubrics, and the presenter recommended that she grade all of the students' responses to each item before moving onto the next item. She was skeptical at first, but decided to try it. She found that by doing this she had a better overall picture of the students' responses for each item and that she graded the students' papers more efficiently. She liked that she did not have to reorient herself to each scoring rubric when she moved on to the next student's test.

Lucia made a time-saving change when she decided to grade all of the students' responses to each item before moving on to the next. This simple change in grading a test can provide teachers with an overall sense of student performance on each short answer and essay item. It also is more efficient in that the teacher has the rubric in front of her as she grades each student's paper and is not switching from rubric to rubric with each new item for each new student. More important, though, Lucia also now grades essay items more reliably.

Care and consideration must be taken into account in both developing a rubric and applying a rubric. The simple guidelines and tips provided help to increase the validity and reliability of short answer and essay items on a test, thereby increasing the validity and reliability of the test itself.

Developing Valid and Reliable Supply-Response Items: A Deliberate Approach

Developing supply-response items requires a deliberate approach and one that includes attention to both the item itself and the anticipated response. In the case of short answer and essay items, the anticipated response is translated into a scoring rubric, which is an essential piece in developing a valid and reliable item. You may be concerned that developing a rubric for each item and scoring each item with a rubric will be time-consuming, and at first it probably will be. However, once a rubric has been created for a specific skill or set of content, it can be used with similar content or skills. The application of a rubric can actually reduce grading time because it focuses the grading of the short answer or essay item.

A test that includes both select-response *and* supply-response items can assess a wide range of content at varying cognitive levels, which is why we advocate the use of different item types on tests, depending on the content and level of cognitive demand required in the curriculum. Choosing the most appropriate item types helps you to create items that assess what you want to assess and that are relatively free from systematic error.

1   Gronlund, N. E. (2006). *Assessment of student achievement* (8th ed.). Boston: Pearson; Hogan, T. P. (2007). *Educational assessment: A practical introduction.* Hoboken, NJ: Wiley Jossey-Bass; Popham, W. J. (2002). *Classroom assessment: What teachers need to know* (3rd ed.). Boston: Allyn and Bacon; Stiggins, R. J. (2005). *Student involved assessment for learning* (4th ed.). Upper Saddle River, NJ: Merrill; Taylor, C. S., & Nolen, S. B. (2005). *Classroom assessment: Supporting teaching and learning in real classrooms.* Upper Saddle River, NJ: Pearson.

2   Bausell, C. V. (2007). State of the states. *Quality Counts 2007: From cradle to grave.* Retrieved May 25, 2007, from http://www.edweek.org/media/ew/qc/2007/17sos.h26.assessments.pdf

3   Bausell (2007).

4   The better item in this example is a released test item from the Washington Assessment of Learning, Grade 5 Science Assessment retrieved May 15, 2007, from http://www.k12.wa.us/assessment/WASL/Sciencetestspecs/pubdocs/G52006ScienceReleaseDocument.pdf

6

Providing Feedback from Tests to Support Student Learning

All children can learn. This is an implicit belief that most teachers share, and it is a belief that should drive all teachers' efforts in the classroom with each and every child, each and every day. There is little, if any, disagreement about that.

But, of course, there are some qualifiers to this belief statement. All children can learn; but children—and adults, too, for that matter—learn in different ways, at different rates, and to different degrees. It is with these ideas in mind that we turn our attention to how teachers can use the results of their classroom-based assessments to support student learning, because these differences concerning *how* people learn suggest that learning is not a one-way process of presenting and receiving. Instead, learning is a reciprocal process, because teaching leads to learning and learning leads to new teaching, and so on.

Assessment is the means through which teachers obtain information about the nature and degree of student learning. Teacher-made tests, in particular, are a way to tap into students' cognitive processes and thereby sample their knowledge, comprehension, and ability to apply, grapple with, and make meaning from their learning in all manner of subject areas. Well-constructed teacher-made tests are a means of making student learning evident so that teachers can make judgments and decisions about student learning and communicate these to others. But, this is an incomplete picture of the role of assessment in teaching and learning.

Learning does not stop with assessment. One might think otherwise, however, when we consider some situations we have seen in our own experiences. Consider, for example, the ninth-grade history teacher who administers a unit test to her students, spends 2 nights at home diligently grading the tests, and hands them back to her students on the third day with final marks of 85, 72, 43, 99, and the like. Incorrect answers are noted with an **X**, and points are deducted from the short answer and essay questions for factual and grammatical errors. As the teacher hands back the grades, she reminds students this was a "major test" and comments, "It's obvious that some of you didn't study the way you needed to." But she adds, "The good news is that several of you aced it!" The teacher concludes by telling students that they must take home their tests for their parents to sign and that everyone who returns the test signed tomorrow will receive 5 extra points on the test. With that, the teacher instructs the students to put their tests in their notebooks and to open up their textbooks to Chapter 8 to begin the next unit.

You probably have some concerns about the teacher's practices in this example. We do, too. Although we commend the teacher for working to grade and return the tests as quickly as she could and for attempting to communicate with parents, we're concerned about the *flat* feedback of the numeric grades, the generalized admonitions about study habits, and the inappropriate use of bonus points. We're also concerned that the teacher seems to tacitly intend for the test to serve as the end mark on the learning associated with the instructional unit. We don't think the teacher means to communicate this, but her actions seem to say, "We've learned—or, in some cases, *not learned*—that material, so now let's move on to new material."

Learning should *not* stop with testing—quite the opposite, in fact. Assessment, as we suggested in the first chapter of this book, is integral to the teaching and learning process. A groundbreaking study by the Assessment Reform Group bears this out. The team of researchers argued that teachers should use a variety of testing measures in the classroom not only as the assessment *of* learning but also as assessment *for* learning. Related to our point at the beginning of this chapter that every child can learn, the Assessment Reform Group posited that the view of assessment *for* learning "is underpinned by confidence that every student can improve."[1]

How, then, are teachers to use their classroom-based, teacher-made tests to support student learning? The answer, in short, is through the effective use of feedback. **Feedback** is specific, understandable information about one's own performance or achievement that can be constructively used to continue and/or to improve learning. In this chapter, we explore the role of feedback in the teaching-learning-assessing process. We first look at the most basic type of feedback teachers can provide on assessments: grades. We then review the expanding research base on the characteristics of effective feedback and specific techniques for providing feedback on teacher-made tests. Finally, we explore the potential long-term outcomes for students that can result when teachers use feedback constructively in their classrooms.

Grading

Grading is the most basic type of feedback that tests provide to students and teachers.[2] In fact, the significance of grading in the minds of students and teachers is evident in the common refrain voiced in classrooms as any given teacher is about to hand back a test to students. "What'd I get?" students are apt to be heard asking.

Whether consciously or unconsciously, students—and even many teachers—seem to consider a test grade the outcome of a transaction within the classroom: You (the teacher) teach me; I (the student) learn; you test me; I get a grade. The grade, therefore, is a representation of the *value* of the learning transaction.[3] Indeed, grading is a type of **evaluation,** which may be defined in the classroom context as a systematic process of making judgments about the nature or worth of student learning. It is important to recognize that grading a test is an evaluative process, because it reiterates the importance of grading in ways that are valid, reliable, and, ultimately, support student learning.

When a grade is put on a test or quiz, the teacher is communicating a judgment about the nature and degree of student learning. Most typically, a test grade is communicated as a percentage correct or a letter grade, but sometimes symbols such as check marks or smiley faces serve as grades, as do numbers such as raw scores. In any case, the function of grading is the same. **Grading** is the translation of student performance on an assessment into a system of relative numbers or symbols to classify and communicate student learning on a given scale. In other words, a grade—whether C, 85, or ☺—is intended to comprehensively represent the nature and degree of a student's learning on a given set of instructional objectives.[4]

How Should Classroom Tests Be Graded?

The number of ways to grade classroom tests is as many as the types of tests that teachers may create. Given this, we address the issue of how to grade a test by exploring two basic principles of grading: validity and reliability. As discussed in Chapter 2, validity and reliability are concepts central to constructing appropriate and fair tests in the classroom. These two concepts are also the central principles for determining how to most fairly and appropriately grade a test.

As a reminder, *validity* is the extent to which inferences drawn from assessment results are appropriate. Therefore, as teachers consider the process of grading a test, they must aim for grading in a way that allows them to make judgments about student learning that are related to the intended objectives of the instructional unit. Similarly, *reliability* is the consistency or dependability of the results of an assessment. Therefore, the teacher must use a grading process that is not unduly influenced by chance or error, either of which would lead to an inaccurate representation of student learning as measured by the test.

In short, the same principles that are used to *construct* a valid and reliable test are used to *grade* the test. With this in mind, Figure 6.1 draws from concepts presented in Chapters 2 to 5 and provides a series of questions that teachers can use to guide their thinking as they consider their own test grading practices.

Figure 6.1. Principles of Grading

Validity	Reliability
1. *Is the assessment (that is, individual test items) adequately aligned with and representative of the instructional objectives?* A grade is not valid if the assessment from which the grade is derived has a low degree of validity.[5] (Refer again to Step 1 of Constructing a Valid and Reliable Test in Chapter 3.)	1. *Is the assessment sufficiently free of systematic error?* (Refer again to Step 6 in Chapter 3, and also to Chapters 4 and 5 on how to construct various test item types.)
2. *Are individual test items weighted to reflect the relative importance of content and skills?* Alternatively (and preferably), are there more test items for instructional objectives of greater importance or emphasis compared to instructional objectives of lesser relative importance or emphasis?[6] (Refer again to the discussion of *content validity* in Chapter 2 and to Step 2 of How to Construct a Valid and Reliable Test in Chapter 3.)	2. *Is there a sufficient number of test items for each instructional objective to reduce the likelihood of error or chance unduly influencing results?* (Refer again to Step 5 in Chapter 3.)
	3. *Will partial credit be awarded on responses; and, if so, what specific criteria will be used?* Whether used for short answer, essay, or computational questions, the partial credit requires that teachers and students have a clear understanding about the expectations for showing work or whatever the criteria may be. (Refer again to the Guidelines for Developing a Scoring Rubric in Chapter 5.)

3. *Will and, if so, how will* implied *and* conditional *content be graded?* For example, will composition, grammar, and mechanics be graded on a science test that includes an essay response? If so, these learning objectives should be explicit. (Refer again to Step 1 of Constructing a Valid and Reliable Test in Chapter 3.)

4. *What relative* number *or* symbol *will the grade take, and will that meaningfully communicate the nature and degree of student learning to others—most importantly, to students?* As a simple example, a ✓ on a unit test would likely be quite insufficient to communicate the degree of a student's learning, whereas a ✓, ✓+, or ✓– may be an adequate means of conveying learning on a single-question, short answer quiz.

4. *Can the grading criteria (including the scoring key and any rubrics) be applied objectively?* Although subjectivity is inherent to the test creation process (for instance, the teacher decides what to assess and how), the grading system should ensure that the teacher's inherent biases or that conditions such as time of day, setting for grading, and so forth, do not influence grades. (Refer again to Step 8 in Chapter 3 and Tips for Applying a Rubric in Chapter 5.)

5. *Will an* item analysis *be used to identify potential systematic error in the test and, if so, will grading of the test be amended accordingly?*[7] An item analysis provides insight into potential error in the construction of test items. (Refer again to Step 10 in Chapter 3.)

The intent of Figure 6.1 is to present a conceptual view of grading as being guided by the familiar principles of validity and reliability. In addition, presentation of nine questions with brief explanations and references back to specific sections in previous chapters is intended to reinforce the centrality of the principles of validity and reliability. Our hope is that teachers can then apply these principles within whatever grading systems, policies, or expectations are characteristic of their particular teaching contexts.

How Can Test Results Be Used to Support Student Learning?

Applying the principles of validity and reliability is the means for determining grades on teacher-made tests. Through grading, teachers and students then have a numeric or symbolic representation of student learning.

But grades themselves are of limited value in terms of contributing to ongoing student learning unless they are translated back into the curriculum from which the test was initially created. Fenwick English, a noted scholar in curriculum, calls this "the reconnect."[8]

We illustrated this in Chapter 3 with the example of a science teacher named Phyllis and her use of an *item analysis* as Step 10 in the process of constructing a valid and reliable test. As suggested by both English's "reconnect" and Phyllis' use of item analysis, the important point is that teachers must analyze students' performance on individual test items and then view the assessment results through the lenses of the curricular objectives. Thus, a teacher moves from viewing test results solely as a list of grades and begins to view test results as a series of *inferences* about student learning.

Let's look at a scenario of Mr. Franks, a high school geography teacher. He has just graded his unit test on sub-Saharan Africa, with which he was assessing students on the following objectives:

- Students will use maps and globes to obtain geographical information.
- Students will identify regional climates and physical characteristics.
- Students will describe how humans influence the environment and how the environment influences people.
- Students will analyze trends in human migration and cultural interaction.
- Students will use geography to interpret, analyze, and make judgments about past and current events.

After grading the students' tests, Mr. Franks sees that the class's grade distribution is 7 As, 9 Bs, 5 Cs, 2 Ds, and no Fs. Although the grades provide a representation of the *degree* of student learning, they provide little in terms of the *nature* of student learning. What's more, the summative grades are not very helpful in informing Mr. Franks' decisions about future instruction. Thus, Mr. Franks analyzes the results by individual test items (that is, he conducts an item analysis), thereby allowing him to draw inferences about student learning in terms of intended curricular objectives. Mr. Franks draws the following conclusions from his analysis:

- All the students are proficient at using maps and globes and identifying regional climates and physical characteristics. (Note: Mr. Franks deemed *proficiency* to mean that a student got most of the questions associated with a particular objective correct.)

- Most students are proficient at describing human and environmental influences, except for Karla, Lori, and Mike. Lori, however, correctly responded to the short answer questions related to this objective, whereas Karla and Mike struggled with both the multiple choice and the short answer questions.

- Approximately half of the students were below proficiency or only marginally proficient in analyzing trends in human migration and cultural interaction. Notably, Mike performed well on this section, whereas Lori did not. Only one student out of the entire class—that was Toni—answered every one of the associated questions correctly. A review of the questions suggested that several of the multiple choice items were missed by most of the class in this section; but, as a whole, students performed better on the short answer questions associated with this objective.

- Most students proficiently responded to the essay question that required students to interpret, analyze, and make judgments about historical and current events using geographical information. Notably, of the two students who earned Ds on the test, Lori's answer was acceptable whereas Mike's was not. More than one-third of the class earned perfect scores on the essay.

Through an analysis of students' performance on test items associated with specific instructional objectives, Mr. Franks is able to draw inferences about the nature of student learning, both individually and collectively. Were Mr. Franks to only consider the grades, he would likely infer that the unit was a success in that everyone passed the test; but he would then miss several important insights into student learning. For example, Lori and Mike earned the lowest grades on the test, but the nature of their performances are *not* the same. Lori appears to have performed relatively well when answering supply-response items, such as short answer and essay questions. She was proficient at interpreting, analyzing, and making judgments about historical and current events using geographical information. Mike, however, seemed to struggle with the written responses but performed notably well on analyzing trends in human migration and cultural interaction. It is only by *reconnecting* students' performance on tests to the curricular objectives from which tests are constructed that teachers can use test results to support student learning.

Formative Feedback

Ultimately, the purpose of assessment in the classroom is to *improve* student learning. Teachers test students so that they can have insight into students' acquisition of knowledge and skills, but such insight is gained only by viewing students' performance through the lens of curricular objectives. The same is true for students. If students only view their test grades as symbols, letters, or percentages that summatively represent their performances, opportunities to support student learning are potentially lost. Students need specific, understandable information about their performances that can be constructively used to continue and improve learning. Such information constitutes **formative feedback.**

As stated previously, grades are the most fundamental and common type of feedback derived from classroom assessments. However, it is important to recognize that grades carry a great deal of baggage with them. Think of how culturally ingrained the scale of A-B-C-D-F is in the United States. In this country, we have a common understanding of what the scale represents: A is excellent; B is good; C is fair; D is poor, but acceptable; and F is unacceptable—a failure. As evidence of the prevalence of this grading system, consider how we apply the scale to practically anything beyond classroom assessments. We say to a companion, "I give that movie a C." Or a parent says to a child, "A+ on tidying your room today." Grades such as C and A+ convey meaning.

What we don't know in these two examples, however, is what made the movie a C and what made the tidying up an A+. If we wish to convey *instructive* meaning about our judgments, we must say something about the expectations or criteria that were met and those that were unmet. (Indeed, simply marking a response right or wrong is negatively correlated with student achievement.[9]) Returning to the previous examples paragraph, the companion explains about the movie, "The acting was good, but the plot was too predictable." Or the parent says to the child, "I appreciate your tidying up your room on your own and that everything is put back in its place. It will make it easier to find your toys, and now there's plenty of room on the floor to play again!" In both cases—the amateur movie critique and the contented parent—the grades are translated into information that makes the expected criteria explicit. This is formative feedback.

Does Formative Feedback Support Student Learning?

The role of formative feedback in supporting student learning has long been established but has gained renewed interest and appreciation in recent years. More than four decades ago, Benjamin Bloom identified the statistically significant effect of feedback in mastery learning, which he and his colleagues documented as contributing to an increase in student achievement of more than one standard deviation compared to conventionally taught students.[10] A review of several studies from the 1970s and the early 1980s also drew affirming conclusions about the power of feedback in the classroom:

- Feedback can promote student learning if students engage with feedback information intentionally.

- Feedback can support student motivation.

- Feedback can promote students' self-monitoring and meta-cognition.[11]

Even more recently, researchers have identified feedback as an essential component of effective teaching. In a meta-analysis of empirically researched instructional strategies, Marzano, Pickering, and Pollock identified *providing feedback* as one of a number of high-yield strategies with a statistically-proven evidence base correlated with improved student learning.[12]

The case for using formative feedback based on classroom assessments has grown still stronger through the work of the Assessment Reform Group in England.[13] Through a series of studies during the past decade, these researchers have established increasing evidence that teachers' formative assessment practices in the classroom can significantly contribute to improved student learning.[14]

What Are the Characteristics of Good Formative Feedback?

In Chapter 1, we defined **teaching** as the intentional creation and enactment of activities and experiences by one person that lead to changes in the knowledge, skills, and/or dispositions of another person, and we defined **learning** as a relatively permanent change in knowledge, skills, and/or dispositions precipitated by planned or unplanned experiences, events, activities, or interventions. These definitions suggest that there is an interaction between the learner and her environment. In a review of literature on the role of feedback in learning, a team of researchers posited this:

Any theory that depicts learning as a process of mutual influence between learners and their environments must involve feedback implicitly or explicitly because, without feedback, mutual influence is by definition impossible. Hence, the feedback construct appears often as an essential element of theories of learning and instruction.[15]

The realization that feedback is central to learning is echoed by other researchers, as well. Consider these statements:

- "Students are high on the list of people who make decisions on the basis of classroom assessment results."[16]

- "The most noble purpose of assessment is to provide feedback to both the student *and* the teacher."[17]

- "Assessment for learning must involve pupils, so as to provide them with information about how well they are doing and guide their subsequent efforts. . . . The awareness of learning and the ability of learners to direct it for themselves is of increasing importance in the context of encouraging lifelong learning."[18]

- "To be effective, feedback should cause thinking to take place."[19]

- "A continuing mission of [formative] assessment should be to help students make more knowledgeable decisions regarding their current tactics."[20]

As illustrated by the preceding comments, feedback is a vital aspect of improving student learning through classroom-based assessments. So, what are the characteristics of good formative feedback? Figure 6.2 presents five essential features of feedback that can support and promote student learning.

Figure 6.2. Characteristics of Effective Formative Feedback[21]

> **Honest**
>
> What does *honest* feedback mean? This criterion almost suggests that a teacher may be *dishonest* or may intend to deceive. We don't think that's likely to happen purposefully among teachers. But, is it possible that feedback may *unintentionally* deceive students? Is it possible that feedback could be *intellectually dishonest*? For example, generic or disingenuous praise (e.g., "Good work") can convey a false sense of mastery to a student who, in fact, has made fundamental and correctable errors in her work. What we are suggesting is that feedback must be *truthful*. It must represent *what is* and not lead to other inferences.
>
> **Accurate**
>
> Accurate feedback is fair.[22] It is, in essence, feedback that is reflective of the learning objectives (i.e., valid) and based on dependable information that is not subject to error or chance (i.e., reliable). Therefore, teachers must clearly know and understand the expected criteria for student performance, and they must use assessments to gather information that provides an appropriate reflection of students' acquisition of the curricular objectives.

Specific

Specific feedback is necessary; otherwise, efforts to support student learning become over-generalized and unfocused.[23] Specific feedback, therefore, is precise and selective, using what evidence is available from test results to target instructional objectives for reteaching, remediation, or other ongoing instructional activities.[24] Specific feedback tends to be more easily understood by students.[25] It is also more germane to criteria of achievement.[26] For example, stock phrases such as "Well done!" and summative letter grades do not communicate specific elements of strength or shortcomings in a student's thinking or application of skills. A comment such as "Remember to provide examples from the text to support your generalization" does. Specific feedback helps to focus on learning objectives.

Constructive

Assessment feedback is strongly associated with student motivation. Feedback, therefore, should be positive in tone.[27] A comment such as "Think about the definition of a control variable; which variable in the experiment fits this definition?" is much more constructive than "You obviously didn't study!" This is *not* to say that feedback should forsake honesty for constructiveness. Rather, by combining honesty, accuracy, specificity, and constructiveness, feedback can provide students with a realistic and feasible sense for *how* to improve learning.

Timely

Feedback must also be timely.[28] In other words, feedback must occur within a timeframe reasonably associated with the assessment activity; otherwise, feedback will lose its relevance. Feedback that is separated from performance by days or even weeks of time (such as often happens with teachers marking major projects or tests and also with most standardized tests) becomes meaningless and, thus, largely useless to students.

It must be noted that these five characteristics of feedback represent distinct, but interrelated, aspects of effective formative feedback. Teachers should understand that, in order for feedback to be used effectively in the classroom to support learning, each of the five characteristics bears importance. It is not enough, for example, to provide accurate and specific feedback. To maximize the instructive effect of feedback, it must also be honest, constructive, and timely. Teachers, therefore, are wise to consider practical ways to provide formative feedback to students in their own classrooms.

How Can I Provide
Formative Feedback to Students?

When the results of classroom-based tests are purposefully employed by teachers to support and promote student learning, then teachers are engaged in using **assessment** *for* **learning.** This turn of phrase is widely used in contemporary educational literature to suggest a distinction from the conventional use of tests in the classroom, namely assessment *of* learning. Assessment *of* learning seeks to determine the nature and degree of student learning, whereas assessment *for* learning is the intentional use of assessment strategies and instruments by teachers with their students to direct and contribute to learning activities.

Assessment for learning is a compelling concept; and, as noted in the earlier review of research associated with feedback, it is a powerful means of supporting student learning. Assessment for learning can occur in the classroom in a variety of ways, including the use of pretests, checking for understanding during instruction, and disaggregating standardized assessment results. However, given the focus of this book, we turn our attention to practical techniques for providing formative feedback to students using the results of teacher-made tests in the classroom. In other words, after a teacher has *administered* and *graded* a class's set of tests, what are some practical approaches for *handing back* and *reviewing* students' assessment results? We explore seven such techniques that are supported by previous research and our own experiences. Note the common theme throughout these seven techniques: To prompt students to think about their own learning.[29]

1. Explain to Students How the Assessment Was Scored[30]

As suggested in the earlier scenarios of the amateur movie critique and the contented parent, summative representations of students' performances on tests (such as percentage scores and letter grades) are of limited value to students. For the results of an assessment to convey instructive information, students must understand the *criteria* by which their performances are assessed. Thus, a simple and effective technique for providing formative feedback to students is to explain to students how the test was scored. For students to make use of feedback, they must know the criteria for expected performance.[31] This can include, for example, reviewing scoring rubrics for short answer, computational, or essay responses. It can also include explaining not only how items on the test are weighted, but why they are weighted in particular ways. For older students, reviewing tables of specifications for tests with their teachers can be a relatively quick and visually intuitive way of conveying the criteria for performance in terms of curricular objectives. This provides students the information necessary to view their test results in specific and constructive ways. We also offer one additional caveat about explaining to students how assessments were scored: It is important to communicate with students about assessment results in language that is familiar to them. This means referring back to specific terms, concepts, facts, or skills from previous instructional activities and doing so in the context of discussing test items and student responses. In this way, assessment results can become reconnected to instruction.

2. Provide an Overview of the Class's Aggregate Performance on the Assessment

First, let us be clear that it is *poor* practice to publicly disclose individual grades on assessments; therefore, our advocating of sharing aggregated results with students should be done in a way that protects students' confidentiality. Otherwise, teachers risk violating the principle that feedback be *constructive*. With that said, it can be highly *instructive* for many students (especially older students) to view their test grades and their performances on individual test items in relation to the performances of other students. Note, though, that the intent is neither to create competition among students nor to shame students into trying harder. The intent, about which teachers must be clear and must clearly convey to their students, is to provide a context for students to interpret their own performances. With this said, the kind of aggregated performance data we recommend sharing includes the following:

- Measures of central tendency on the assessment, such as mean, median, and mode
- The range of scores on the assessment
- The item analysis, including indications of the averages of partial credit on computational items and on criteria identified with scoring rubrics for short-answer or essay responses

When presented for purposes of providing students a relative sense for their performance, such data can allow students to identify specific strengths or weaknesses. Such information also provides an honest and forthright sense of achievement. We caution, however, that this technique can be unintentionally misused if teachers forget to attend to the need for feedback to be *constructive*.

3. *Limit the Amount of Feedback Provided to Students*

A practical reality in many classrooms is that time is a rare commodity. It is, therefore, not always feasible to orally review tests with a class comprehensively, question by question. This is not necessarily a bad thing, however. Research on feedback has shown that the sheer *amount* of feedback is not correlated with increased student achievement.[31] Therefore, an effective technique for providing formative feedback is to limit the amount of feedback. Teachers should concentrate on essential understandings rather than elaborating on details or information that is "nice to know," as suggested by Wiggins and McTighe's instructional planning approach known as Understanding by Design.[32] The same holds true for providing written feedback. By providing a limited amount of focused feedback both to individual students and to whole classes, teachers are attending to the feedback principle of *specificity*. What's more, by giving less attention to the comprehensiveness of feedback, teachers are able to provide greater *depth* of feedback, an approach that supports the *constructiveness* of the feedback for students.

4. *Provide Written and Oral Commentary First, Then Provide the Grade at a Later Time*

A common phenomenon when handing back assessment results in a classroom is that students immediately look at the grade. Then, any written feedback that is provided on the assessment—whether simple indications of multiple choice questions that are incorrect or extensive written commentary on an essay response—is viewed through the lens of the summative grade. A practical technique to mitigate this phenomenon is to return assessments with written and oral commentary but not with summative grades. This practice helps engage students in the feedback and to interpret their own performances in light of the feedback rather than through the lens of the grade. Feedback is generally more effective if it is accompanied by explanation, but the explanation can be lost if it is overshadowed by a summative grade.[33] As a variation on this technique, teachers can provide written or oral commentary first, and then require students to respond (in writing or orally) before receiving the grade.[34] Such techniques are particularly effective when providing feedback on short-answer and essay responses, especially if students have their teacher's written feedback and a rubric with which to review their own writing. Feedback is then more *specific* and *constructive* because it is interpreted by the students.

5. *Give Students the Opportunity to Ask Questions*

Whether providing written feedback, oral feedback, or a combination of both, it is important to provide students with the opportunity to ask questions. A common error that teachers make, however, is to provide insufficient time for students to *think* before asking their questions. Providing feedback too quickly—that is, before students are prompted to and have the opportunity to reflect on their performance themselves—can actually dampen, if not preclude, the potential positive effects of feedback on learning.[36] Therefore, teachers should precede an invitation to ask questions with a structured time for students to review and reflect on written and oral feedback, such as described in technique #4. Then, during the time available for question and answer, teachers should consider some possibilities for the best way to allow for questions, while balancing the constraints of time and the fact that taking time to answer an individual student's question may or may not be helpful to the rest of the class. For example, as suggested in techniques #2 and #3, teachers can use their item analyses to frame which test questions to review. In this way, teachers retain some control over time in class, while also serving the needs of a larger proportion of the class. As time allows, individual questions can be addressed. Also, depending on class sizes and the types of assessment items (such as a heavy use of supply-response items), teachers may consider individually conferencing with students. In instances when teachers of high school students use extended written responses on assessments and individual conferencing is *not* planned, teachers may invite students to ask about their written responses, but let them know in advance that they (that is, the teachers) may need to reread the response to provide students the best feedback possible. This is because it can be quite difficult to recall the intricacies of one essay out of a class or 25, not to mention several classes of 25 students each. The use of the techniques associated with prompting student questions about their assessment performances can support the use of feedback that is *honest, specific, constructive,* and *timely.*

6. *Allow for Student-to-Student Discussion*

An effective means of informal formative assessment within classrooms is teacher-facilitated discussion. This instructional strategy can be adapted for providing formative feedback to students using results from classroom-based assessments. Marilyn Burns suggests five ways to prompt and facilitate student-to-student discussion, and the following list is adapted from her ideas:

1. Ask students to explain their answers, whether or not the answers are correct.

2. Ask students to share their solution strategies with the group.

3. Call on students who don't volunteer or whose thinking must be made evident.

4. Organize small groups to review specific test items, being sure to provide directions for which items to review, how to review them, and how to report to the larger group.

5. Ask students to restate others' ideas.[37]

There are at least three distinct advantages to using student discussion to review formative feedback on assessments. First, students often benefit from engaging with other students in a structured, collaborative activity. In other words, students can effectively learn from each other.[38] Second (and related to the first point), helping others to learn can reinforce one's own learning. Third, student discussion provides teachers excellent opportunities to identify the nature of students' thinking and possible misunderstandings, thereby providing teachers with richer information from which to make instructional decisions.[39] Indeed, for teachers who intentionally listen to what students are saying to each other during collaborative reviews of assessments, student discussions can provide a number of *teachable moments* of which teachers can take *timely* and *constructive advantage*.

7. *Provide the Opportunity to Redo or Revise*

Feedback is most effective when it allows students to reengage with the content and skills associated with a particular test item, series of items, prompt, or extended assessment. As suggested in the previous six techniques for providing formative feedback, teachers can reengage students in a number of ways, all intended to get students thinking. However, there is evidence that feedback becomes even more powerful when it is *applied*. Schmoker argues, for example, that "Students need . . . feedback—and they need it quickly, with the opportunity to correct or revise."[40] Black and his research associates recently concluded that "Comments become useful feedback only if students use them to guide further work, so new procedures are needed."[41] Indeed, the idea of providing students the opportunity to rewrite essays or retake entire tests is new to many teachers or, at least, an idea that is somewhat uncomfortable to consider. Nevertheless, it is an idea that strongly reflects the notion that the ultimate purpose of assessment is not grading, but *improving student learning*. Here's how one practicing teacher illustrated his insight into using formative feedback to provide students opportunities to reengage with the content and skills of his curriculum, rather than focusing solely on grades:

If students are allowed to raise their grade through extra-credit work that is independent of essential learning, then that raised grade reinforces the view of grades as a commodity to be earned. When a student asks for an extra-credit assignment to raise his or her grade, I remind the student that the purpose of grades is to assess and promote learning. A low grade simply communicates a learning gap; the way to raise the grade is to learn more. I explain that although I do not believe in extra credit, I do believe in opportunities for further learning. A student who scored low on a formal paper, for example, may seek extra writing help, rewrite the paper, and try for a higher grade. If a student received a low quiz grade, he or she may take the quiz again to demonstrate mastery of the material. This approach helps reinforce the view that grades are a communication tool, not the goal.[41]

Summing Up What We Know About Providing Feedback

Using formative feedback from classroom-based assessments can be a powerful instructional tool for teachers. The seven techniques described earlier provide practical and proven ways to help teachers harness the potential to use assessments *for* learning. However, teachers must exercise considerable professional judgment when planning for providing formative feedback to students. For example, teachers are wise to consider their students' ages, grade levels, and learning needs when deciding what techniques or variations of techniques to use. Teachers should also consider differences in the use of these techniques among various subject areas. Although feedback is positively correlated with student learning in all core subject areas, the specific demands of providing feedback on essay responses in an English class differ from those required of a series of computational problems in a physics course.[42]

Regardless of the specific techniques that teachers use to provide formative feedback, the guiding principle remains the same: *To prompt students to think about their own learning*.[43] More specifically, teachers' intentions should be to guide students to answer three essential questions, based on the formative feedback given to them:

1. What have I set out to learn?
2. How am I progressing?
3. What do I need to do to continue my progress?[44]

Therefore, a teacher's feedback—be it written or oral, presented to the class or individually—should provide students insight into the answers for these questions.

Fostering Students' Abilities to Self-Assess: The Tacit Outcomes of Feedback

Formative feedback is, indeed, a powerful means of supporting and improving student learning. This is certainly important for the immediate and short-term objectives associated with formal curricula in typical courses of study. For example, formative feedback can help students improve their understanding of historical facts, their application of the order of operations in solving equations, their composition of persuasive essays, or their analysis of data tables. But students' frequent and ongoing engagement with formative feedback can lead to longer-range outcomes, as well.

Figure 6.3 presents five long-range outcomes for students that can be collectively described as *assessment as learning*. Assessment *as* learning suggests a distinction from both assessment *of* learning and assessment *for* learning. The term **assessment *as* learning** refers to students' disposition for and ability to self-assess and, ultimately, to self-direct learning.

Figure 6.3. Tacit Long-Range Learning Outcomes: Assessment *as* Learning[46]

By engaging with formative feedback frequently and over time, students will be able to:

- ✓ Accurately articulate criteria of achievement, learning, and success
- ✓ Ask meaningful questions as a means of learning
- ✓ Constructively provide feedback to others
- ✓ Effectively respond to feedback from others
- ✓ Actively reflect on learning

Assessment *as* learning suggests that one of the larger aims of formal education is to enable students to become *lifelong learners,* capable of formulating and pursuing interests and needs associated with continuous learning well beyond the twelfth grade. This long-range curricular aim is articulated by many educators.

- ◆ We must constantly remind ourselves that the ultimate purpose of evaluation is to enable students to evaluate themselves. Educators may have been practicing this skill to the exclusion of the learners. We need to shift part of this responsibility to students. Fostering students' ability to direct and redirect themselves must be a major goal—or what is education for?

Art Costa[47]

- [One of the key, empirically supported factors for using assessment-related techniques to improve student learning is] the active involvement of pupils in their own learning . . . and the need for pupils to be able to assess themselves and understand how to improve.

Assessment Reform Group[48]

- Only by abdicating some control in the classroom can teachers empower students to monitor and make decisions about their own learning. . . . If students are to become reflective practitioners and autonomous learners, they must be given opportunities to develop these skills.

Butler & McMunn[49]

- Many teachers who have tried to develop their students' self-assessment skills have found that the first and most difficult task is to get students to think of their work in terms of a set of goals. Insofar as they do so, they begin to develop an overview of that work that allows them to manage and control it for themselves. In other words, students are developing the capacity to work at a metacognitive level.

Black, Harrison, Lee,
Marshall, & Wiliam[50]

- Teaching students to assess their own work helps them better understand the skills that are valued in a particular field and develop the general life skills of being able to look honestly at and improve their own work.

K. McGonigal[51]

- Assessment *as* Learning is the ultimate goal, where students are their own best assessors.

Lorna Earl[52]

As we consider the intention that the inclination and ability to self-assess are important, longer-term aims of formal education, it is interesting to note how the three fundamental elements of formal education become conjoined. *Assessment as learning* brings together curriculum, instruction, and assessment. Thus, assessment cannot be thought of as *that thing teachers do at the end of instruction* and that is *done to students* at the end of instruction. Instead, assessment itself becomes an important component of our teaching and an important learning tool for our students.

1   Assessment Reform Group. (1999). *Assessment for learning: Beyond the black box* (p. 7). Cambridge: University of Cambridge School of Education.

2   Bangert-Downs, R. L., Kulik, C. C., Kulik, J. A, & Morgan, M. (1991). The instructional effect of feedback in test-like events. *Review of Educational Research 61*(2), 213–238.

3   Brown, F. G. (1981). *Measuring classroom achievement.* New York: Holt, Rinehart, and Winston.

4   Gronlund, N. E. (2006). *Assessment of student achievement* (8th ed.). Boston: Allyn & Bacon.

5   Butler, S. M., & McMunn, N. D. (2006). *A teacher's guide to classroom assessment: Understanding and using assessment to improve student learning* (p. 151, 153). Hoboken, NJ: John Wiley & Sons; Gronlund (2006).

6   Ory, J. C., & Ryan, S. E. (1993). *Tips for improving testing and grading.* Newbury Park, CA: Sage.

7   Airasian, P. W. (2005). *Classroom assessment: Concepts and applications* (5th ed., p. 317). New York: McGraw-Hill.

8   English, F. W. (2000). *Deciding what to teach and test: Developing, aligning, and auditing the curriculum* (p. 19). Thousand Oaks, CA: Corwin Press.

9   Bangert-Downs, Kulik, Kulik, & Morgan (1991).

10   Bloom, B. (1984). The search for methods of group instruction as effective as one-to-one tutoring. *Educational Leadership, 41*(8), 4–17.

11   Bangert-Downs, Kulik, Kulik, & Morgan (1991).

12   Marzano, R. J., Pickering, D., & Pollock, J. (2001). *Classroom instruction that works.* Alexandria, VA: Association for Supervision and Curriculum Development.

13   Assessment Reform Group (1999).

14   Black, P., Harrison, C., Lee, C., Marshall, B., & Wiliam, D. (2004, September). Working inside the black box: Assessment for learning in the classroom. *Phi Delta Kappan, 86*(1), 9–21.

15   Bangert-Downs, Kulik, Kulik, & Morgan (1991), p. 214.

16   Stiggins, R. J., & Conklin, N. F. (1992). *In teachers' hands: Investigating the practices of classroom assessment* (p. 184). Albany: State University of New York Press.

17   Wilson, L. W. (2005). *What every teacher needs to know about assessment* (2nd ed., p. 100). Larchmont, NY: Eye On Education.

18   Assessment Reform Group (1999), p. 7.

19   Black, Harrison, Lee, Marshall, & Wiliam (2004, September), p. 14.

20   Popham, W. J. (2008). *Classroom assessment: What teachers need to know* (5th ed., p. 275). Boston: Allyn & Bacon.

21   Adapted from Assessment Reform Group (1999).

22 Stiggins & Conklin (1992), p. 143.

23 Brown (1981), p. 171.

24 Butler & McMunn (2006), p. 141.

25 Butler & McMunn (2006), p. 141.

26 Stiggins & Conklin (1992), p. 143.

27 Brown (1981), p. 171.

28 Brown (1981), p. 171.

29 Assessment Reform Group (1999).

30 Hogan, T. P. (2007). *Educational assessment: A practical introduction.* Hoboken, NJ: John Wiley & Sons.

31 Wilson (2005).

32 Bangert-Downs, Kulik, Kulik, & Morgan (1991).

33 Wiggins, G., & McTighe, J. (2005). *Understanding by design, expanded* (2nd ed.). Alexandria, VA: Association for Supervision and Curriculum Development.

34 Bangert-Downs, Kulik, Kulik, & Morgan (1991).

35 Black, Harrison, Lee, Marshall, & Wiliam (2004, September).

36 Bangert-Downs, Kulik, Kulik, & Morgan (1991).

37 Burns, M. (2005). Looking at how students reason. *Educational Leadership 63*(3), 26–31, 29–30.

38 Marzano, Pickering, & Pollock (2001).

39 Ory, J. C., & Ryan, S. E. (1993). *Tips for improving testing and grading.* Newbury Park, CA: Sage.

40 Schmoker, M. (2006). *Results now: How we can achieve unprecedented results in teaching and learning* (p. 169). Alexandria, VA: Association for Supervision and Curriculum Development.

41 Black, Harrison, Lee, Marshall, & Wiliam (2004, September), p. 13.

42 Winger, T. (2005). Grading to communicate. *Educational Leadership 63*(3), 61–65, 64.

43 Bangert-Downs, Kulik, Kulik, & Morgan (1991).

44 Assessment Reform Group (1999).

45 Assessment Reform Group (1999); Chappuis, J. (2005). Helping students understand assessment. *Educational Leadership 63*(3), 39–43.

46 See Assessment Reform Group (1999); Black, Harrison, Lee, Marshall, & Wiliam (2004, September); Chappuis (2005); King, J. (2007, May 9). The high stakes in science education: Risking the roots of American productivity. *Education Week.* Retrieved June 1, 2007, from http://www.edweek.org/ew/articles/2007/05/09/36king.h26.html? print=1, ¶ 10–14; Leahy, S., Lyon, C., Thompson, M., & Wiliam, D. (2005). Classroom assessment: Minute by minute, day by day. *Educational Leadership 63*(3), 18–24; Earl (2003); Stiggins, R. J. (1999, November). Assessment, student confidence, and school success. *Phi Delta Kappan*, 191–198; Stiggins, R. (2005, December). From formative

assessment to assessment FOR learning: A path to success in standards-based schools. *Phi Delta Kappan,* 324–328.

47   Costa, A. L. (1989). Re-assessing assessment. *Educational Leadership, 46*(7), 2–3.

48   Assessment Reform Group (1999), p. 5.

49   Butler & McMunn (2006), p. 151, 153.

50   Black, Harrison, Lee, Marshall, & Wiliam (2004, September), p. 14.

51   McGonigal, K. (2006, Spring) "Getting More 'Teaching' out of 'Testing' and Grading." *Speaking of teaching, Center for Teaching and Learning, 15*(2), 3. Retrieved from May 7, 2007, from http://ctl.stanford.edu/ Newsletter/testing_grading.pdf

52   Earl, L. (2003). *Assessment as learning: Using classroom assessment to maximize student learning* (p. 25). Thousand Oaks, CA: Corwin Press, p. 25.

7

How Can I Constructively Influence Professional Practice in My School?

The answer to the title of this chapter is twofold: by developing the competency of assessment and then by becoming a teacher-leader in the area of assessment. Throughout this book, we have emphasized and drawn on an understanding that assessment is integral to teaching and learning. Whereas *curriculum* identifies the knowledge and skills students are intended to acquire and *instruction* provides the means by which students engage with these objectives, it is the role of *assessment* to ascertain the nature and degree of students' learning. Furthermore, it is from assessments of learning that teachers and students can then make informed decisions about past experiences, current needs, and future learning activities.

Given the important role of assessment in teaching and learning, it is vital that teachers possess and apply the knowledge, skills, and dispositions associated with this professional competency. When teachers gain these, they can serve both formally and informally as leaders in their schools to improve the assessment practices of their colleagues.

Assessment as a Professional Competency

In Chapter 1, we reviewed the licensure requirements of a number of states, which suggested a widespread appreciation of the importance of assessment within the profession. However, the descriptions of assessment as a professional competency vary considerably among state licensure requirements; therefore, we offer here a summary of our view of the three essential aspects of the professional competency of assessment. In brief, teachers must be good *creators of, consumers of,* and *communicators about* assessment.

Teachers Must Be Effective Creators of Assessments

Even in a standards-based curriculum, in which the learning objectives for students are articulated within state curricular frameworks, it is the role of classroom teachers to translate standards into accessible and relevant instruction for students. In other words, curriculum and instruction must necessarily be particularized by teachers for the students they teach any given academic year. Consequently, teachers must also particularize assessment—that is, they must be able to develop assessments of student learning that are not merely reflective of the standards-based curriculum for which they are accountable, but assessments that are responsive to *how* and *how much* they have taught. This is not easily accomplished by simply lifting a commercially produced test from a textbook series, from test-generating software, or released test items from the state department of education. Rather, teachers themselves must be able to *create* assessments that are fair to students, are feasible to employ in the classroom setting, have practical purpose regarding continued student learning, and result in accurate indications of student performance.[1] This is not to say that outside resources cannot be integrated into teacher-made tests; they can, if checked for validity and reliability.

In addition (and as suggested again and again by teacher licensure standards and professional literature), teachers must be able to create *a variety of assessments* appropriate to the grade level of students and for the subject matter being taught. The variety of assessments can include quick checks for understanding in the midst of instruction, quizzes to inform student progress and highlight areas of need, and tests to gauge cumulative learning over some period of time. Furthermore, the variety of assessment types may range from select-response items such as true-false, matching, and multiple choice, to supply-response items such as computational questions, short written answers, extended essays, or even projects, performances, or original creations. Teachers must master certain knowledge and skills to effectively create assessments to collect information about student learning in their classrooms. For example, teachers must understand and be able to apply the principles of validity and reliability, create tables of specifications, select and construct different types of assessment items, and analyze assessment results to make instructional decisions. These topics, of course, have been the focus of this book (Chapters 2–6 in particular), and we highlight them here as a reminder of the specialized knowledge and skills associated with effective and appropriate assessment practices in the classroom.

Teachers Must Be Intelligent Consumers of Assessments

A central purpose of assessment is to collect information about student learning. But, too often in classrooms, the outputs from assessments follow a very predictable path. For example, students take a test, the teacher grades it, the students receive the test back, and a grade is entered in the grade book. In this common scenario, information about student learning is collected; but it is used primarily—if not solely—as a source for a grade.

It is incumbent on teachers not only to gather information about student learning, but also to meaningfully interpret that information, both for individual students and in the aggregate for classes. Assessment information can be used to identify patterns of strengths and struggles among students, within specific content strands, and with various levels of cognition.

Understanding the purpose and structure of the assessment itself is a critical step in interpreting and *consuming* the information about student learning that the results of a quiz, a test, a project, or any other type of assessment can provide. But this is not only true for teacher-made assessments in the classroom. It is equally important that teachers be able to interpret and use the results of standardized assessments. These results can provide critical information regarding the progress of the class toward meeting the standards required by the state. However, being handed reams of student score reports (as is oftentimes the practice these days) is insufficient for making *data-driven decisions* about student learning, as we would want teachers to do. One problem with the standardized assessment results is that a reconnect to specific state standards is not made from these assessment results.[2] A teacher may receive information that a student has reached a certain achievement level, but specific curricular objectives may not be evident. Again, as with teacher-made assessments, a first step for the teacher in interpreting and using standardized test results is to understand the purpose and structure of the test itself. Teachers must be intelligent *consumers* of assessments and the information about student learning that both teacher-made and standardized assessments can provide. Here are three fundamental cautions that teachers should keep in mind regarding state standardized assessments:

- *State assessments are well-suited for drawing inferences about the achievement of populations but not particularly well-suited for drawing inferences about individual students' learning.* State standardized assessments are less reliable indicators of *individual achievement* because such assessments typically assess a large number of curriculum objectives with a relatively small number of questions; and state assessments usually represent an individual's performance on a given day, without repeated measures. For these reasons they tend to be less reliable indicators of individual achievement than they do as indicators of a group's achievement.

◆ *State assessments tend to be well-aligned with curriculum state standards, but they may not assess some important objectives from the local curriculum.* For example, oral language skills, such as public speaking, are often integral to the English/Language Arts curriculum; however, state assessments do not assess this important strand of learning objectives simply because oral language is not readily assessable in a standardized testing format. Teachers must be cautious of drawing sweeping inferences about student learning in the absence of evidence about objectives that are not tested.

◆ *State assessments assess higher-order thinking but* not *the highest levels of cognition.* State standardized assessments have been criticized for being nothing more than simple tests of recall. However, this is not the case. Most state assessments assess higher-order thinking beyond recall, such as *comprehension, application,* and even *analysis.* Nevertheless, a fairer criticism of standardized assessments is that they do not tap the *highest levels* of cognition, namely synthesis and evaluation. The reason for this is evident in Chapter 4: Most state standardized tests use multiple choice format, which can efficiently assess a broad range of learning objectives, but has limited ability to assess the *highest levels* of cognition. Therefore, many important curricular objectives that include students' abilities to synthesize and evaluate simply are not assessed on state tests.

Classroom teachers create assessments to gauge their students' learning and use the results of commercially produced tests to inform their teaching. Therefore, teachers should be good *consumers* of assessment results both from their own classroom-based assessments (as described in Chapter 6) and from standardized assessments.

Teachers Must Be Effective Communicators About Assessments

The acts of creating assessments and of interpreting assessment results are very much within the purview of teachers. However, assessment results—that is, information that represents the nature and degree of student learning—is not of interest only to teachers. Other people involved in the educational process have strong interests in assessment results as well, namely, students, parents, and other educators. Yet *why* teachers communicate about assessment with these other people is different. Let's consider the essential purposes of communication about assessment for each of these groups.

Why should teachers communicate about assessment with students? The primary purpose must be to support and improve student learning by providing feedback, as described in Chapter 6. When a teacher shares assessment results with students intentionally and conscientiously, that feedback *about* student learning can become a powerful instructional strategy to support student learning.[3] In addition, students need to know where they stand in terms of summative evaluations of their learning. The fact remains that test scores, course grades, grade point averages, and the like *mean something*. They are intended to communicate the worth or value of student achievement, and such grades are used by teachers, students, and others to make decisions. Therefore, summative indications of student learning must be communicated, as well.

Why should teachers communicate about assessment with parents? Again, as with providing feedback to students, the ultimate aim of communicating about assessment with parents is to support and improve student learning. Parents are the first and most important teachers of their children. Therefore, it is incumbent on teachers to provide useful information about student learning to parents in the most constructive ways feasible. That means, for example, that teachers may need to translate assessment results from *educationese*—the jargon-laden language of our profession that we're comfortable speaking among ourselves as educators, but which may be unhelpful, if not inaccessible, to the typical parent. It may mean that teachers should rely less on the age-old convention of A-B-C-D-F to communicate the degree of student learning and more specifically talk about a student's competencies in, for example, composing essays and spelling, and a weaknesses in sentence construction and sentence variety. In other words, teachers must consider ways to provide feedback from assessments that is less summative in favor of providing information that is more formative. This is information about student learning that parents can better understand and, therefore, potentially use to support their children's learning.

Why should teachers communicate about learning with other educators? There are a host of reasons:

◆ *Principals and other building-level instructional leaders* use assessment results from teachers to monitor student learning, to identify patterns of strengths and weaknesses among students, and to provide an important additional perspective on student learning that standardized assessments cannot offer. In other words, wise instructional leaders value and use classroom-based assessment results as valid and reliable information about student learning and, therefore, the effectiveness of educational programs in the school.

- *Teachers in the next grade level* use the previous year's or previous semester's assessment results as the initial and important indicator of a student's prior achievement and, therefore, of their current knowledge and skills. Teachers can then begin to plan for instruction based on valuable assessment data.

- *Guidance counselors* at all school levels use classroom assessment results to help students and families make decisions about courses of study and future educational paths.

- *Child study teams* use classroom assessment results to help make decisions about interventions or services that may be necessary and important support for individual students.

- *Program coordinators, honors committees, and admissions committees* use classroom assessment results (namely in the form of course grades and grade point averages) as important factors in making decisions about entry into educational programs, awards and recognitions, as well as for entry into post-secondary education.

Teachers communicate information about student learning to a number of people—namely, students, parents, and other educators—for a number of reasons. This fact suggests one clear need: The information that teachers communicate about student learning must be information that is appropriate and accurate. If assessment information is inappropriate and inaccurate, people's impressions and decisions about student learning will be misguided and maybe even harmful.

Assessment is integral to the process of teaching and learning. Indeed, assessment is the means by which teachers can determine the nature and degree of student learning and through which instructional decisions can be knowledgeably and effectively made. It is imperative, therefore, that every teacher exhibit competency in *creating, consuming,* and *communicating about* student assessment and learning. This has been our primary aim throughout this book. More specifically, we hope to help teachers improve their ability to assess student learning in their classrooms in ways that are valid, reliable, meaningful, and, ultimately, supportive of student learning.

Teacher Leadership: Constructively Influencing the Professional Practice of Others

Being able to create, use, and communicate about student learning through meaningful assessment practices in the classroom is central to what it means to teach. As teachers individually develop and master the competency of assessment, we believe it is incumbent on those teachers to help lead other teachers to do the same. The act of teachers serving as leaders to other teachers is known as **teacher leadership,** which we define as the constructive influence of one teacher on the professional practice of one or more other teachers. Within the professional domain of classroom assessment, there are several ways that teachers can positively contribute to the improved practice of their colleagues.

Lead by Example

First and foremost, teachers influence the practice of other teachers through their own examples. Therefore, a first step in teacher leadership around the competency of assessment is to create, use, and communicate about assessment in ways that are *legally responsible, feasible, useful,* and *accurate* (these being the essential facets of good assessment practices as described in Chapter 2). Teachers lead by their spoken and observed example, whether in the classroom, teachers' lounge, or any other settings in which teachers are engaging with each other. Demonstrating principles of assessment through one's own professional practice can be a powerful motivator for other teachers to want to learn more and to improve on their own skills.

Collaborate With Other Teachers

An increasingly recognized means of professional development is through teacher collaboration. In Japan, for example, educators have demonstrated notable success with the use of *lesson study.* In a lesson study, a team of teachers jointly plans for a lesson or a series of lessons on a topic. Then one of the teachers delivers the planned lesson in his or her classroom while the other teachers on the study team observe. Following the demonstration lesson, the entire team of teachers critiques the design and efficacy of the lesson itself (as opposed to the focusing on the particular teacher's delivery of the lesson). Through this approach, the team of teachers develops a series of collaboratively designed and proven lessons.

Teachers can take a similar approach in the area of assessment. Collaboratively designed assessments can be powerful tools in supporting grade levels, departments, or interdisciplinary instructional teams to develop shared assessments ranging from quizzes to unit tests to benchmark tests to end-of-course tests to culminating performances. Whatever the level of assessment, the creation of collaboratively designed and constructed assessments requires a team of teachers to jointly unpack the shared curriculum, identify essential understandings, select the means of assessing student learning, recognize the inherent limitations of the assessment, and thereby be better prepared to interpret and use the results of the common assessment.

Advocate for Professional Development in the Area of Assessment

As described in the opening chapter of this book, the assessment practices of many teachers in today's schools have been developed inconsistently at best and haphazardly at worse. Our concern from our own experiences both with and as classroom teachers is that classroom-based assessment is an extraordinarily important component of teaching and learning that has long received insufficient attention. Although our suspicion is that this has been the case for decades, the current era of standards-based accountability has brought the situation to light. In short, many teachers need support in developing their professional competencies in the domain of assessment. Therefore, teacher leaders can constructively influence the professional practice of other teachers by advocating for and, indeed, by providing professional development opportunities in assessment.

It is worth noting that this book has sought to present a case for improving teachers' classroom-based assessment abilities, but that professional development in assessment can go still further. For example, the principles and techniques of assessment described in this book are generic to students in elementary, middle, and high schools. However, the specific application of the principles of assessment vary for students of different ages. Targeted professional development can address this important point. Similarly, the application of the principles of assessment vary for different subject areas.[4] Teachers must have *pedagogical content knowledge* to be effective classroom teachers, meaning that teachers must have a combination of depth of subject matter and depth of understanding about how best to teach that subject. Pedagogical content knowledge should include practical understandings of common errors and difficulties in the subject area, as well as the ability to interpret and respond to individual students' difficulties in learning the subject area, which are made evident through appropriate assessments germane to the subject.[5]

Teaching is a profession, which suggests that the act of teaching requires the ongoing exercise of learned decision-making to anticipate, respond to, and meet the needs of learners. Thus, professional development within the important domain of assessment is imperative for teachers throughout their service in classrooms.

Constructively Develop and Critically Review Assessments Used by School Districts

School districts are increasingly promoting the use of benchmark tests to assess student learning. **Benchmark tests** are assessments of student achievement intended to indicate progress toward the acquisition of a set of learning objectives that will be summatively assessed on a subsequent test. In practical terms, school districts and schools increasingly encourage or require teams of teachers to develop common benchmark assessments (also called *short-cycle assessments*). However, a critical error that we have seen repeated in many school settings is that benchmark tests are being created by teams of teachers ill-prepared to design and construct such assessments, resulting in teachers throughout entire schools, and often entire school districts, using benchmark tests that have low degrees of validity and reliability.

With this concern in mind, here are some practical questions to address when collaboratively designing, constructing, and planning to use school- and district-level benchmark tests:

- What are the intended purposes of benchmark tests?
- When will benchmark tests be used in relation to summative assessments?
- Will benchmark tests sample the same objectives assessed by state standardized assessments, or will benchmark tests assess curricular objectives more comprehensively?
- Will benchmark tests assess all the objectives that are assessed by the subsequent standardized tests, or will benchmark tests assess only the objectives expected to have been taught and acquired according to the available pacing guide at the time of the benchmark testing?*

- Will benchmark tests mimic the format of state standardized tests to provide students experience with that format?
- How much instructional time will be needed to administer benchmark assessments?
- How and by whom will benchmark tests be scored?
- In what format (e.g., grades, scaled scores, percentages, curricular strands) and to whom will results be communicated?
- Will teachers be held accountable for their students' test results?
- Will students be held accountable for their test results (e.g., will they receive a *grade*)?
- Will teachers be expected to use benchmark test results to plan instruction? If so, in what format will results be made available to teachers?

Inform Policy Regarding the Use of Assessment in the Classroom

As we have suggested previously, much of what many teachers know about assessment has been learned through their own experiences both as former students themselves and as practicing teachers. How, then, are assessment policies in schools, districts, and states developed? One study concluded, "Often, testing and grading policies are written by educators who have little formal background in sound assessment practice. This can lead to the implementation of policies that can have a detrimental influence on the nature and quality of classroom assessment."[6]

Policy is developed to express the beliefs of an organization and to guide the work of the professionals within that organization. Policies regarding assessment practices are found at all levels of the K–12 educational system, including the school, district, and state levels. Given this fact, teacher leaders can constructively influence the professional practice of other teachers by using their understanding of the principles of classroom-based assessment to inform school and district policies. For example, does a school require that certain types of assessments be used by teachers, such as quizzes, tests, and projects, or does the school require that grades be assessed and reported by objectives rather than by types of assessments? Does the school mandate the relative percentages that each of these types of assessments is worth in calculating a final grade? Does the school have a traditional letter-grade scale, or does the school use a developmental rubric? Does the school have a homework completion policy or a provision for not assigning zeros for assignments that students do not complete?

Although the number of policies that may govern assessment in schools is myriad, our point here is that teachers who have developed competencies associated with appropriate classroom-based assessment principles can and should use their knowledge to inform the practices of others. Contributing to the development, review, and revision of policy is a powerful means of promoting best practices within the domain of assessment.

Summing Up Teacher Leadership of Assessment

By providing an example of professional competency in the domain of assessment, collaborating with others to construct assessments, advocating for teachers' ongoing professional development, and influencing policy, teacher leaders constructively influence the professional practice of others in their schools and school districts. The longer-range aim of such efforts is to change the culture of assessment within the profession. In other words, by positively contributing to the improved practice of other teachers, teacher leaders can change the way that assessments—whether teacher-made or standardized—are viewed and used by teachers. The intended effect of this is that teachers are more willing and more able to discern the nature and degree of their students' learning; to draw more valid and reliable inferences about their students' learning; and, therefore, to better make instructional decisions about what to teach and how to teach, thereby resulting in improved student learning. Through improved assessment practices in the classroom, teachers are better able to link curriculum and instruction in the service of student learning.

1   Joint Committee on Standards for Educational Evaluation. (2003). *The student evaluation standards.* Thousand Oaks, CA: Corwin.

2   English, F. W. (2000). *Deciding what to teach and test: Developing, aligning, and auditing the curriculum.* Thousand Oaks, CA: Corwin Press.

3   Marzano, R. J., Pickering, D., & Pollock, J. (2001). *Classroom instruction that works.* Alexandria, VA: Association for Supervision and Curriculum Development.

4   Brown, F. G. (1981). *Measuring classroom achievement.* New York: Holt, Rinehart and Winston.

5   Black, P., Harrison, C., Lee, C., Marshall, B., & Wiliam, D. (2004, September). Working inside the black box: Assessment for learning in the classroom. *Phi Delta Kappan, 86*(1), 9–21.

6   Stiggins, R. J., & Conklin, N. F. (1992). *In teachers' hands: Investigating the practices of classroom assessment* (p. 185). Albany: State University of New York Press.

Glossary of Terms

accuracy standards one of four domains of the Student Evaluation Standards, the accuracy standards are professional criteria requiring that teacher-made assessments provide appropriate and dependable information about student learning to facilitate the education process

analytical rubric a scoring key that provides information regarding performance in each of the component parts of a task, making it useful for diagnosing specific strengths and weaknesses

assessment the process of using methods or tools to collect information about student learning

assessment as learning students' dispositions for and ability to self-assess, and, ultimately, to self-direct learning

assessment for learning the intentional use of assessment strategies and instruments by teachers with their students to direct and contribute to learning activities

benchmark tests assessments of student achievement intended to indicate progress toward the acquisition of a set of learning objectives that will be summatively assessed on a subsequent test

checklist a list of behaviors or look-fors in a supply-response item

concurrent validity the degree to which two assessments administered within a given time period and that presume to measure the same learning outcomes correlate in their results

conditional content specific circumstances, context, or conditions under which and/or materials with which the student will engage with the explicit content

consequential validity the appropriateness of the intended and unintended outcomes that ensue from an assessment

construct validity how accurately an assessment aligns with the theoretical framework of the intended learning outcomes, standards, or objectives of the instructional unit

content the subject matter to be delivered

content validity how adequately an assessment samples the intended learning outcomes, standards, or objectives of an instructional unit

criterion validity how accurately an assessment equates with another assessment that is intended to measure the same learning outcomes, standards, or objectives

curriculum a set of intentionally identified outcomes of learning*

error when an assessment item inadequately distinguishes between the student who has truly mastered the intended learning outcome and the student who has not

explicit content subject matter directly referred to in a standard or learning objective

evaluation a systematic process of making judgments about nature or worth of student learning

face validity "the appearance of validity"**

feasibility standards one of four domains of the Student Evaluation Standards, the feasibility standards are professional criteria requiring that teacher-made assessments be realistic in their intent and design so that they can be used in actual classroom settings

feedback specific, understandable information about one's own performance or achievement that can be constructively used to continue and/or to improve learning

formative assessment the assessment of student learning integrated into the act of teaching

formative feedback specific, understandable information about student performance that can be constructively used to continue and to improve learning

grading the translation of student performance on an assessment into a system of relative numbers or symbols to classify and communicate student learning on a given scale

holistic rubric a defined level of expected performance on a supply-type item that is applied to a student's overall performance but is not indicative of specific components of the performance

implied content prior knowledge and skills students need to engage in the explicit content of the curriculum

instruction planned and unplanned experiences provided by a teacher that are intended to result in the acquisition of a set of intended learning outcomes by students

---

*   Johnson, M. (1967). Definitions and models in curriculum theory. In Ornstein, A.C., & Hunkins, F. P. (2004). *Curriculum: Foundations, principles, and issues* (4th ed., p.180). New York: Pearson.
** Angoff, W. H. (1988). Validity: An evolving concept. In Wainer, H., & Braun, H. I. (Eds.) *Test validity* (p.23). Hillsdale, NJ: Lawrence Erlbaum Associates.

inter-rater reliability the consistency with which two or more scorers apply the grading criteria of an assessment thereby resulting in stable assessment results among students, uninfluenced by factors that are not the intended criteria of learning

intra-rater reliability the consistency with which a scorer applies the grading criteria of an assessment, thereby resulting in stable assessment results uninfluenced by factors that are not the intended criteria of learning

learning a relatively permanent change in knowledge, skills, and/or dispositions precipitated by planned or unplanned experiences, events, activities, or interventions

level of cognitive demand expected level of thinking when engaged with specific content

predictive validity the degree to which the results of one assessment can foretell results on another assessment that is intended to measure the same learning outcomes, standards, or objectives

preassessment assessment of student learning prior to teaching

propriety standards one of four domains of the Student Evaluation Standards, the propriety standards are professional criteria requiring that teacher-made, classroom-based assessments be legal, fair, and do no harm to students

random error error that influences assessment results but is not controllable

reliability the consistency or dependability of the results of an assessment

scoring rubric a description of the nature of an acceptable response

select-response items items that have predetermined responses from which the student must choose

summative assessment assessment of student learning at the end of some period of instruction

supply-response items assessment items for which the student must provide the answer

systematic error error that is unintentionally built into an assessment, but which may be controlled when detected

table of specifications a chart or table that details the content and level of cognitive demand assessed on a test as well as the types and emphases of test items

teacher leadership the constructive influence of one teacher on the professional practice of one or more other teachers

teaching   the intentional creation and enactment of activities and experiences by one person that lead to changes in the knowledge, skills, and/or dispositions of another person

test   a deliberately designed, representative set of written questions and/or prompts to which students respond in written form, intended to measure the acquisition of certain knowledge, skills, and/or dispositions

unpacking the standards   the process of reviewing curricular objectives to identify the intended content and cognitive levels of learning for students

utility standards   one of four domains of the Student Evaluation Standards, the utility standards are professional criteria requiring that teacher-made assessments have practical use in the classroom that supports student learning

validity   the extent to which inferences drawn from assessment results are appropriate

Appendix

The Student Evaluation Standards[*]

Propriety Standards   The propriety standards help ensure that student evaluations will be conducted legally, ethically, and with due regard for the well-being of the students being evaluated and other people affected by the evaluation results. These standards are as follows:

P1   **Service to Students** Evaluations of students should promote sound educational principles, fulfillment of institutional missions, and effective student work, so that educational needs of students are served.

P2   **Appropriate Policies and Procedures** Written policies and procedures should be developed, implemented, and made available, so that evaluations are consistent, equitable, and fair.

P3   **Access to Evaluation Information** Access to a student's evaluation information should be provided, but limited to the student and others with established legitimate permission to view the information, so that confidentiality is maintained and privacy protected.

P4   **Treatment of Students** Students should be treated with respect in all aspects of the evaluation process, so that their dignity and opportunities for educational development are enhanced.

P5   **Rights of Students** Evaluations of students should be consistent with applicable laws and basic principles of fairness and human rights, so that students' rights and welfare are protected.

---

[*]   Joint Committee on Standards for Educational Evaluation. (2003). *The student evaluation standards.* Thousand Oaks, CA: Corwin.

P6	**Balanced Evaluation** Evaluations of students should provide information that identifies both strengths and weaknesses, so that strengths can be built upon and problem areas addressed.
P7	**Conflict of Interest** Conflicts of interest should be avoided, but if present should be dealt with openly and honestly, so that they do not compromise evaluation processes and results.

Utility Standards   The utility standards help ensure that student evaluations are useful. Useful student evaluations are informative, timely, and influential. Standards that support usefulness are as follows:

U1	**Constructive Orientation** Student evaluations should be constructive, so that they result in educational decisions that are in the best interests of the student.
U2	**Defined Users and Uses** The users and uses of a student evaluation should be specified, so that evaluation appropriately contributes to student learning and development.
U3	**Information Scope** The information collected for student evaluations should be carefully focused and sufficiently comprehensive, so that evaluation questions can be fully answered and the needs of the students addressed.
U4	**Evaluator Qualifications** Teachers and others who evaluate students should have the necessary knowledge and skills, so that evaluations are carried out competently and the results can be used with confidence.
U5	**Explicit Values** In planning and conducting student evaluations, teachers and others who evaluate students should identify and justify the values used to judge student performance, so that the bases for the evaluations are clear and defensible.
U6	**Effective Reporting** Student evaluation reports should be clear, timely, accurate, and relevant, so that they are useful to students, their parents/guardians, and other legitimate users.
U7	**Follow-up** Student evaluations should include procedures for follow-up, so that students, parents/guardians, and other legitimate users can understand the information and take appropriate follow-up actions.

Feasibility Standards The feasibility standards help ensure that student evaluations can be implemented as planned. Feasible evaluations are practical, diplomatic, and adequately supported. These standards are as follows:

F1	**Practical Orientation** Student evaluation procedures should be practical, so that they produce the needed information in efficient, nondisruptive ways.
F2	**Political Viability** Student evaluations should be planned and conducted with the anticipation of questions from students, their parents/guardians, and other legitimate users, so that their questions can be answered effectively and their cooperation obtained.
F3	**Evaluation Support** Adequate time and resources should be provided for student evaluations, so that evaluations can be effectively planned and implemented, their results fully communicated, and appropriate follow-up activities defined.

Accuracy Standards The accuracy standards help ensure that a student evaluation will produce sound information about a student's learning and performance. Sound information leads to valid interpretations, justifiable conclusions, and appropriate follow-up. These standards are as follows:

A1	**Validity Orientation** Student evaluations should be developed and implemented, so that interpretations made about the performance of a student are valid and not open to misinterpretation.
A2	**Defined Expectations of Students** The performance expectations of students should be clearly defined, so that evaluation results are defensible and meaningful.
A3	**Context Analysis** Student and contextual variables that may influence performance should be identified and considered, so that a student's performance can be validly interpreted.
A4	**Documented Procedures** The procedures for evaluating students, both planned and actual, should be described, so that the procedures can be explained and justified.

A5 **Defensible Information** The adequacy of information gathered should be ensured, so that good decisions are possible and can be defended and justified.

A6 **Reliable Information** Evaluation procedures should be chosen or developed and implemented, so that they provide reliable information for decisions about the performance of a student.

A7 **Bias Identification and Management** Student evaluations should be free from bias, so that conclusions can be fair.

A8 **Handling Information and Quality Control** The information collected, processed, and reported about students should be systematically reviewed, corrected as appropriate, and kept secure, so that accurate judgments can be made.

A9 **Analysis of Information** Information collected for student evaluations should be systematically and accurately analyzed, so that the purposes of the evaluation are effectively achieved.

A10 **Justified Conclusions** The evaluative conclusions about student performance should be explicitly justified, so that students, their parents/guardians, and others can have confidence in them.

A11 **Meta-Evaluation** Student evaluation procedures should be examined periodically using these and other pertinent standards, so that mistakes are prevented or detected and promptly corrected, and sound student evaluation practices are developed over time.

Note: The overview of the Student Evaluation Standards originally published by Corwin Press in 2003 is not copyrighted, and the Joint Committee encourages reproduction and dissemination of the standards as presented. Please see the original source in this reference citation for additional, important information.